D1096291

paper illuminated

paper illuminated

INCLUDES 15 PROJECTS FOR MAKING HANDCRAFTED LUMINARIA,
LANTERNS, SCREENS, LAMPSHADES, AND WINDOW TREATMENTS

HELEN HIEBERT

PHOTOGRAPHS BY BEN FINK

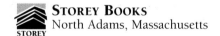

STOREY BOOKS
North Adams, Massachusetts

LIBRARY
OREGON COLLEGE OF ART AND CRAFT
8245 S.W. BARNES ROAD
PORTLAND, OREGON 97225

r by Zelda Tanenbaum

The mission of Storey Publishing is to serve our customers by publishing practical information that encourages personal independence in harmony with the environment.

Edited by Deborah Balmuth and Karen Levy
Designed by Vertigo Design, New York
Photographs on pages viii (bottom), 91, 120, and 122 by Giles Prett; on pages viii (top) and 35
    from the Research Institute of Paper History & Technology; and on pages v, 34, 66,
    and 91 by James Chase
Art direction by Cynthia N. McFarland and Alison Lew
Production assistance by Jennifer Jepson Smith
Illustrations by Elayne Sears except those on pages 122 and 125 (bottom) by Robert Strimban
Indexed by Word·a·bil·ity
Text and templates on pages 84-87 excerpted by permission from *The Papermaker's Companion*, by Helen Hiebert
    (Pownal, VT: Storey Books, 2000:175-177). Text on pages 8 (sidebar) and 106-112 excerpted by permission from
    Lampshades: Basic Wraparound Construction and Cut and Pierced, by Bee Ormsbee and Scott O. Kenyon (Concord,
    NH: The Lamp Shop, 2000:4-22). Safety information on pages 116-119 reprinted by permission from Brian
    Queen from a letter that originally appeared in *Hand Papermaking Newsletter,* 49 (2000): 1-2. Illustrations on
    pages 122 and 125 (bottom) and text on pages 123-126 excerpted by permission from *Antiques on the Cheap*, by
    James W. McKenzie (Pownal, VT: Storey Books, 1998:142-145).
On location photography taken at the Emerson Inn & Spa, 146 Mount Pleasant Road, Mount Tremper, NY, 12457,
    (845) 688-7900, www.the-emerson.com.

Copyright ©2001 by Helen Hiebert

All rights reserved. No part of this book may be reproduced without written permission from the publisher, except by
a reviewer, who may quote brief passages or reproduce illustrations in a review with appropriate credits; nor may any
part of this book be reproduced, stored in a retrieval system, or transmitted in any form or by any means—electronic,
mechanical, photocopying, recording, or other—without written permission from the publisher.

The information in this book is true and complete to the best of our knowledge. All recommendations are made without guarantee on the part of the author or Storey Books. The author and publisher disclaim any liability in connection
with the use of this information. For additional information, please contact Storey Books, 210 MASS MoCA Way,
North Adams, MA 01247.

Storey Books are available for special premium and promotional uses and for customized editions. For further information, please call Storey's Custom Publishing Department at (800) 793-9396.

Printed in Hong Kong by C&C Offset Printing Co., Ltd.
10 9 8 7 6 5 4 3 2 1

LIBRARY OF CONGRESS CATALOGING-IN-PUBLICATION DATA

Hiebert, Helen, 1965-
    Paper Illuminated: includes 15 projects for making handcrafted luminaria,
lanterns, screens, lampshades, and window treatments / by Helen Hiebert.
        p. cm.
    ISBN 1-58017-330-6
    1. Paper work. 2. Lamps. 3. Lampshades. I. Title.

TT870 .H517 2001
745.54--dc21
                                                              2001020071

TO TED

acknowledgments

I am grateful to all of the creative souls who were willing to share their stories, ideas, techniques, and inspirations with me. Special thanks to Jenny Pinto for assisting me in making most of the projects for this book; to Scott Kenyon at The Lamp Shop for allowing me to use her detailed instructions for wraparound shades; and to Brian Queen for sharing his knowledge of lamp safety with me. Thank you mom and dad for being so supportive of my career. Your encouragement and loving support has made it a much smoother ride in so many ways.

thanks

Many thanks to the following contributing artists:
Laura Donnelly Bethmann, Béatrice Coron, Amanda Degener, Andrew Elliott, Ming Fay, Barbara Fletcher, Liz Galbraith, Mary Ginn, Kyoko Ibe, Lanie Kagan, Paula Beardell Krieg, Susan Kristoferson, Brent Markee, Diane Maurer-Mathison, Chris Palmer, Jenny Pinto, Janet St. Cyr, Zelda Tanenbaum, Ruth Timm, Douglas Varey, Nancy Welch, Jennifer Morrow Wilson, Paul Wong, and Therese Zemlin.

Many thanks to the Emerson Inn & Spa, Mount Tremper, New York, for the generous use of their facility while photographing this book.

"Light is immaterial. You grab it with your mind, your soul, your heart. I think of it as a friendly ghost that surrounds us."

INGO MAURER, CONTEMPORARY LIGHTING DESIGNER

contents

Introduction viii

Enhancing Paper 1

Selecting Paper and Art Materials
Making Paper More Translucent
Adding Color
Adding Texture and Dimension

Paper and Candlelight 22

Pop-Up Lantern
Shadow Lantern
Votive Cover

Paper and Natural Light 40

Horizontal Accordion Blind
Vertical Accordion Blind
Pocket Shade
Room Divider
Japanese-Style Screen

Paper and Incandescent Light 68

Luminaria
Spinning Lantern
Chochin Lantern
Night-Light
Wall Sconce
Panel Lampshade
Wraparound Shade

Lamp Basics 114

Safety
Types of Lightbulbs
Lamp Bases
Wiring and Rewiring Lamps

Appendix 127

Glossary of Terms
Patterns
Contributing Artists
Recommended Reading
Supply Sources

Index 134

traditions of paper and light

For millennia, cultures throughout the world have celebrated paper and light. Paper and light combine the functional with the decorative, providing a practical necessity, evoking a mood, and illuminating works of art. Paper can be illuminated with candlelight, natural light, and, more recently, incandescent light. In all cases, the paper diffuses the harshness of the light, giving it a warm, soft glow. In return, the light enhances the paper, displaying delicate and subtle textures, colors, designs, and variations in opacity.

In Japan, *shoji* screens, or wooden panels covered with paper, provide a privacy barrier but allow light to penetrate. In Northern New Mexico, luminaria made from candles anchored in sand-filled bags line rooftops and driveways during festive occasions. In Asian countries, elaborately decorated paper lanterns are used in celebrations to honor Buddha and ancestral spirits. During the festival of the full-moon day in Myanmar, fire balloons as tall as three stories are launched to celebrate Buddha's descent back to earth. These cleverly constructed armatures, shaped like balloons and animals, are sent aloft via fire as the source of hot air (figure 1). Fire balloons are also a tradition in Mexico.

Paper-lantern festivals are also held all over the world to celebrate various occasions. In Germany, when the days grow short in November, residents celebrate St. Martin's Day. Schoolchildren march through the streets carrying handcrafted candlelit paper lanterns, which illuminate the night (figure 2, lantern by Riethmüller GmbH). On August 1st in Switzerland (Independence Day), it is a tradition to hang paper lanterns outdoors. During the annual crayfish festival in Sweden, residents hang paper lanterns in the shape of the sun and the moon. Lantern festivals in the United States include Illumination Night, which is celebrated on Martha's Vineyard, and the Feast of Lanterns, which is held in Pacific Grove, California.

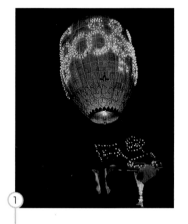

paper and light today

The popularity of combining paper and light, as well as many of the designs for paper lanterns, has its roots in Japan. In 1951, the mayor of a small town in Japan, which was known for making paper lanterns, asked Isamu Noguchi, probably the world's best-known paper lamp designer, to do something to revive the town's sagging economy. He designed the *Akari* hanging lamp, a collapsible paper lampshade that has become popular around the world (figure 3, two of Noguchi's designs). His work has influenced many other contemporary lighting designers and inspired more than one hundred versions of his original design.

Today, paper is gaining in popularity as a beautiful decorative element for lampshades, window treatments, and festive-lighting accessories. More and more shops are springing up, totally devoted to handmade paper and paper crafts. Never before has the selection of unique, handcrafted paper been so extensive or so readily available.

This book will lead you on an exploration of the many ways that you can use paper and light to enhance one another. Take a moment to think about all of the paper paraphernalia that you've enjoyed, such as piñatas, flags, lanterns, and banners. You don't need to relegate these gorgeous objects to only special occasions. If you are like me, you can finally "get rid of" those beautiful papers you've been storing for years and create exquisite, functional objects with them. Rekindle that old paper flame and make illuminated paper a part of your every day décor.

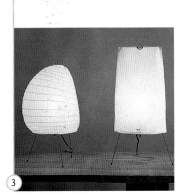

3

enhancing

paper

There are many fabulous papers on the market that can be used for home décor projects. Some papers are translucent, diffusing soft light. A light source shining through them can also show off a subtle pattern in the paper.

When shopping for paper for a lighting project, hold it up to the light. In some cases, illumination can bring it to life. On the other hand, irregularities, uneveness, and other flaws may be visible in a sheet that looks great flat on the rack.

Even though so many beautiful papers are out there, I still love to experiment with decorative techniques to create unique paper with just the design and color I need. There are a variety of ways to enhance a paper's translucent qualities. Let your imagination run wild. I hope you'll enjoy experimenting as much as I have.

selecting paper and
art materials

The paper used for the projects in this book varies
slightly, and I describe the materials you'll need in

each chapter. Before you get started, though, there are a couple of things you

should think about when selecting the paper and art materials you will use.

lightfastness

Some papers and art materials fade over time when exposed to light, be it electric or natural light. Ask your supplier about lightfastness when purchasing paper and art supplies. This is just something to consider; the fading may actually be a very nice touch.

paper grain

Mass-produced paper is made on a conveyor belt, and the fibers are distributed in one direction, which becomes the grain direction of the paper. Since the fibers are more or less aligned in one direction, the paper will fold more easily with the grain. If you fold a paper against the grain, it can crack and become brittle and unattractive.

Paper can be referred to as short grain or long grain; the terms indicate the alignment of the overall sheet. For example, if the grain in an 8½- by 11-inch sheet of paper runs in the 8½-inch direction, it is called short grain. There are several simple techniques to determine the grain direction. One is to fold a small swatch of the sheet of paper, first in one direction and then in the other. The direction in which it folds the cleanest is the direction of the grain.

paper types

Use a paper with sizing (a substance added to some papers to make them more water-resistant) if you'll be applying ink, watercolor, or anything else that bleeds. Your paper supplier can tell you whether a paper is sized or not. If you'll be dampening the paper, it needs to have wet-strength (the ability to accept dampness gradually, rather than absorb it like a paper towel) and it shouldn't tear easily when you pick it up. High wet-strength papers include commercial printing papers, artist drawing or printmaking papers, and handmade papers.

paper weight

There are two basic types of paper: text weight and cover weight. Text-weight paper is generally used for the pages in books, magazines, and brochures. Cover-weight paper is heavier, like card stock, and is used for brochures and paperback book covers. For certain applications, such as origami, you'll need to use thin, text-weight paper; for others, including piercing or embossing, you'll need stiffer, cover-weight paper.

right and wrong sides

Usually, a sheet of paper has a right side (the side that will be seen on the outside) and a wrong side (the other side). For the most part, this will be obvious. If it isn't, it probably doesn't matter, but you may want to make a little mark to indicate which side is going to be the right side. In some cases, two adjoining panels will look different if the right side is showing on one and the wrong side is showing on the other.

adhesives

Some glues dry slower than others, allowing more time in which to work. If you are concerned about the longevity of your projects, you can use archival glues, such as polyvinyl acetate (PVA), which is packaged under several brand names. Some glues are reversible, which means they can be unstuck at a later date, if necessary. A glue stick is handy for some projects, such as gluing paper to paper (I prefer the UHU brand, which is acid free).

Double-sided tape is great for some projects and is available in an acid-free form. It is a bit more expensive, but it doesn't yellow over time as other tapes do. For some projects, superglue or spray mount works best, even though their permanence is questionable.

coloring agents

Use paints and inks that are lightfast whenever possible (Golden acrylic paint is one that I recommend). If you choose a transparent rather than an opaque paint, the color or white of the paper will shine through and contribute to the overall effect. Higgins is an ink brand that is both waterproof and lightfast and comes in a variety of colors. Ask your art supplier for other recommendations.

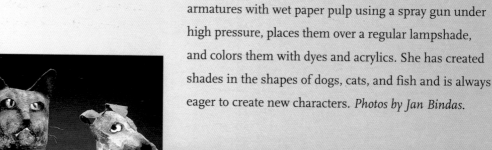

barbara fletcher

Barbara Fletcher, of Boston, Massachusetts, creates her clever, wire screen armatures in animal forms. She then plasters the armatures with wet paper pulp using a spray gun under high pressure, places them over a regular lampshade, and colors them with dyes and acrylics. She has created shades in the shapes of dogs, cats, and fish and is always eager to create new characters. *Photos by Jan Bindas.*

making paper
more translucent

Following are ten ways to enhance the translucency
of paper to make it more visually exciting. Many of

the techniques are quite simple, such as punching and piercing. The

possibilities are endless—trying a few of the suggested techniques will

certainly give you ideas for creating some styles of your own.

batiking

Batiking is traditionally done on fabric, but you can create equally beautiful batiked papers using wax to enhance a paper's translucency (figure 1). Apply melted paraffin, batik wax, or beeswax to your paper with a variety of applicators, such as brushes, cookie cutters, and batik tools, and then brush a wash of liquid dye or watercolor over the wax designs. The waxed areas will be the original paper color, and everywhere else will be the color of your dye.

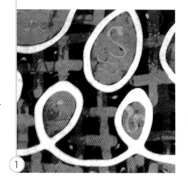

Create another wax design to keep some areas of your paper the new color, and then apply a second dye color. Start with light colors and build up to dark ones. Three to four layers should suffice. Let the dye dry between applications. When you're done, place the batiked paper between sheets of newsprint and iron it to remove the excess wax. Thorough descriptions for this technique can be found in *Paper Art,* by Diane Maurer-Mathison (see Recommended Reading).

cut and pierced

You can create your own designs or find patterns at The Lamp Shop (see Supply Sources) or local craft shops. I recommend practicing this process on scrap paper before making the actual shade. When you feel comfortable, photocopy the image to enlarge it.

Place a piece of carbon or transfer paper on the wrong side of your decorative paper. Position the design over the carbon paper and trace it to transfer the image onto the other piece of paper. Place a piece of cardboard underneath the transferred design and poke through each dot with the piercing tool, piercing through the paper, straight down into the cardboard. Next, place the design on a cutting mat and use a craft knife to cut the straight and curved lines. Erase all pencil lines with an art eraser.

a brief history of the cut-and-pierced technique

The Aladdin kerosene lamp was introduced to the United States in the early 1900s. It shed a much brighter light than previous kerosene lamps and was quite popular. Expensive glass shades were available to diffuse the glare created by the Aladdin lamp, which most rural American families could not afford. As a result, Yankee ingenuity led to the birth of the parchment paper lampshade in New England. Victorian paper crafts (paper cutting, piercing, embossing, and reposée) were popular at the time, and lampshade makers began to incorporate those techniques into their shades. Such lamps were large, and the shades sat on a tripod, which kept them away from the flame.

To open the straight line cuts, insert a small piercing tool all the way into one end of the line and draw the tool along the line to the other end. To mold the curved lines, gently push the loose, curved sections of the design from the right side toward the wrong side of the paper. Do not crease or fold the paper. Turn the work over and gently mold and form the sections inward using your fingertips. Hold your work up to the light periodically to check your progress. These shades are typically lined with a backing paper to prevent direct glare from the bulb through the slits (figure 2).

dripped and ironed beeswax

This technique is most dramatic if you start with an opaque sheet of paper. Light a bleached beeswax candle and hold it over the paper at an angle. When it starts to drip, move the candle over the paper in one-inch increments, letting it drip onto the paper to create a polka dot pattern. The wax will dry momentarily in small lumps. Place the paper between sheets of newsprint and iron it (I use a spare iron, since some wax residue gets onto the iron). The iron melts the wax into the paper, enhancing its translucency and bringing out a polka dot pattern (figure 3). You can also experiment with other dripping designs.

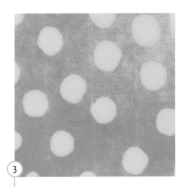

layering

Layering papers can have some interesting effects. Try layering two colors—when illuminated they will blend together to produce a third color. The lamp will look different when it is on and when it is off. If you use layers of the same paper, the layering will not be visible when the lamp is off (especially if you do the layering on the inside of the shade), but the layering will appear when the lamp is on (figure 4, paper by Béatrice Coron).

oiled paper

This old-fashioned technique can be used to enhance the translucency of almost any sheet of paper (figure 5). Apply mineral, tung, linseed, or Danish oil to a sheet of paper with a paintbrush and let the oil soak into the paper for at least 12 hours. Try tinting the oil with an oil-based stain to vary the color or applying the oil with a small brush to create an interesting patterned effect. When you are done, apply three coats of finishing spray or varnish to protect the oil from collecting dirt and dust.

4

5

janet
st. c

For the past 15 years, Janet St. Cyr,
of Webster, New Hampshire, has been
creating lampshades using the traditional cut-and-pierced
method. She has a variety of patterns that customers can
choose from, including flowers, moons and stars, a covered bridge, wheat, and pinecones. *Photo by Ben Fink.*

paper cutting

You can cut anything from simple to exquisite designs in
paper (figure 6, paper by Béatrice Coron). Using a craft knife
for precision, cut freehand or trace an image, which you can
find in clip-art books and magazines. For most projects, you
will need to line the inside of the shade with another sheet of
paper to hide the glare of the bulb.

piercing

Use an awl, needle, or other sharp implement to create small
holes in a sheet of paper for light to pass through. Pierce freehand or affix a pattern to the paper with tape. Place the paper
on top of a piece of cardboard and pierce through the paper
into the board below. Or run the paper through an unthreaded
sewing machine, varying the stitch for different patterns. Fold
the paper into an accordion and run two layers through the
sewing machine to get a symmetrical pattern. Piercing works
best with lightweight card stock and with solid-colored papers
(figure 7, paper by Jenny Pinto).

6

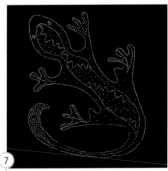

7

printed vellum

Small sheets of printed vellum can be found in many art and craft stores (figure 8). These can be fun to use for small illuminated paper projects.

punching

A variety of punches are available on the market today, and the options are ever changing. Small punches do not have much of a reach, so you are limited to punching within an inch or so of the border of your paper (figure 9). Try punching through pleated paper to get to the center of your work. There are also various punches that simulate die-cutting tools and reach deeper into the paper. Of course, you can be creative and cut your own designs with a craft knife.

scratch-through crayon and acrylic

This technique creates a wonderful effect similar to that of a stained-glass window. Use crayons to cover the entire sheet of paper in any fashion. I like to do a random scribbling pattern of different colors in one-inch-square sections. Brush acrylic paint (black creates a dramatic effect) over the entire surface, so that none of the crayon is visible. After the paint is dry, scratch the surface with a scraping tool, such as a potter's needle or a craft knife, to remove areas of black paint and let the color show through (figure 10, paper by Jenny Pinto).

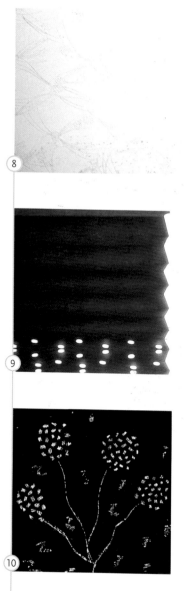

adding color

Following are twelve ways to play with the color of paper to make it more interesting. Some of the

techniques are quite simple, while others are more involved. Have fun

experimenting to get just the right shade and combination of colors that

you want.

Papers by Nancy Welch and Diane Mauer-Mathi

collages

Glue cutouts, decorative papers, photographs, stamps, and other objects onto paper to make a unique design (figure 1).

crayon batiking

I learned this batiking method from Paula Beardell Krieg, and it produces awesome results. Color a high wet-strength piece of paper with crayons, making sure that the entire sheet is covered. Wet the paper and wad it into a tight ball. Make an effort to crease and crinkle it all over, but take care not to rip it. Carefully unfold and lay the sheet on a flat surface. Brush slightly thinned acrylic paint over the entire surface of the sheet, then sponge off the paint. The paint will seep into the creases in the paper, giving it the look of batik (figure 2). To flatten your paper, cover the entire sheet with a clean piece of paper and iron it until it is dry.

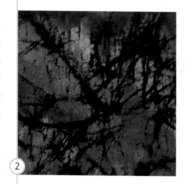

fold and dye

The fold-and-dye technique, called *Itajame,* is a common Japanese dyeing method. Fold a sheet of absorbent paper with a high wet-strength into accordion pleats (thin handmade and Japanese papers work well; Sumi-e is one brand I particularly like). Dip the paper into a container of water and then blot it dry with a towel or a paper towel. Next, dip the corners or the edges of the damp paper into a container of calligraphy ink, fiber-reactive dye, or cold-water dye. The damp paper will help draw the ink up the edges of the paper folds, creating a unique effect (figure 3, paper by Susan Kristoferson).

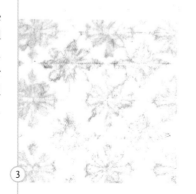

Try varying your pleating and dipping methods to achieve a range of results. Experiment with redyeing a previously dyed sheet or apply dye with an eyedropper rather than dipping it. To avoid staining yourself and your workspace, wear rubber gloves and cover your work surface with plastic cloth and newspaper. Be careful with wet, dyed paper, as it is very fragile. You may need to leave it folded until it has dried.

marbling

Marbled paper has been around for ages. *Suminagashi*, the oldest form, began in Japan or China more than 800 years ago and is a water-based marbling method. Oil-marbled paper, perhaps more easily recognized by its swirling patterns, was used extensively by 18th-century European artisans to create end papers and cover papers for their handmade books. Hand-marbled and commercially marbled papers can be purchased in art stores (figure 4, paper by Diane Maurer-Mathison). Instructions for both marbling techniques can be found in *Paper Art* (see Recommended Reading).

4

marbling with bubbles

This is a fun marbling variation that I learned from artist Paula Beardell Krieg. Make a solution of one part dishwashing liquid to four parts water and add a densely colored water-based paint or ink. Pour the mixture into a flat pan. Using a straw, blow bubbles into the mixture until the bubbles rise above the edge of the container. Lay a piece of paper on top of the bubbles, then remove it from the tray (figure 5, paper by Paula Beardell Krieg).

5

marbling with chalk

Paula Beardell Krieg also taught me this simple marbling technique. Use a knife to scrape colored chalk onto the surface of water in a pan or tray. (Make sure the pan is larger than the sheet of paper you are marbling.) Lay the sheet of paper on the surface of the water briefly, and then lift it out of the water. The chalk color will transfer to the paper. When the paper is dry, cover it with a piece of wax paper, and then cover the wax paper with a piece of clean paper. Iron the stack of paper to transfer the wax onto the chalk-marbled paper to seal it (figure 6, paper by Paula Beardell Krieg).

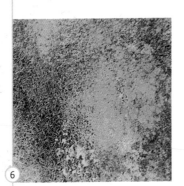

6

nature printing

Nature printing is a way to recreate images from the natural world. Natural objects, including plants, flowers, fruits, vegetables, shells, and feathers, can be inked and printed on paper, fabric, and other surfaces (figure 7, paper by Laura Donnelly Bethmann). There are entire books on how to print with plant matter. Check out *Nature Printing,* by Laura Donnelly Bethmann (see Recommended Reading).

paste paper

There are many recipes for paste, but here is my favorite. Dissolve ½ cup each of rice and wheat flours in one cup of water. Bring four cups of water to boil, then add the dissolved flour solution and stir until it thickens and clears. Remove the pan from the heat. Let it cool, then add acrylic paint to the paste to get the desired color.

Next, spray, paint, or dip a sheet of paper in water to dampen it and place it on a flat work surface. Paint the paste onto the paper in any pattern desired, using one or more colors. Create a pattern on the paper by dragging a comb, rubber stamp, or faux wood-grain tool through the paste before it dries (figure 8, paper by Diane Maurer-Mathison). Hang the paper up or lay it flat to dry.

Jennifer Morrow Wilson, of Little Deer Isle, Maine, created her *Sunrise Table Lamp* (4.5 in. x 6.5 in. x 30 in.) by sewing together pieces of paper that she made herself. The pieces are "quilted" in a way, and the pierced holes made by the stitching allow light to shine through, creating a unique effect. *Photo by Ken Woisard.*

7

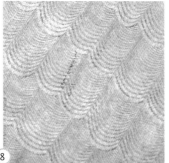

8

rubber stamping

Rubber stamping has become quite popular over the past few years. You can find lots of cool items in stamp stores, including embossing powders, decorative punches, and stamping inks. Stamps can be purchased in any shape or size or you can carve your own from raw carrots and potatoes. You can also use found objects, special rollers, and various block-printing methods, such as linoleum and woodblocks (figure 9). For more stamping and printing ideas, consult *Paper Art* or a local stamp shop.

rubbing

This technique allows you to reproduce textured surface designs right onto a sheet of paper (figure 10, paper by Nancy Welch). Place the paper over a fibrous, rough, or grainy surface, such as leaves, a manhole cover, wood, or anything else you can think of. Use the long side of a crayon, a soft pencil, or graphite and rub over the textured surface. If desired, apply a wash of watercolor or India ink over the rubbing. Apply a coat of clear fixative to prevent smudging.

stenciling

There are many ways to create patterns on paper with stencils. You can use ready-made stencils found in craft or home decorating stores, or you can make your own designs by tracing or photocopying images from books and magazines. Plastic translucent materials, such as stencil acetate or mylar, work best for making stencils, since you can trace original designs through them and they'll hold up for repeated use. Acrylic, oil-based, and water-based paints work well, as do paint sticks (available at craft stores) made specifically for stenciling.

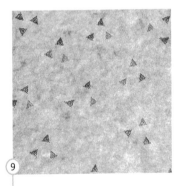

9

10

Tape the stencil in place on the paper. Apply color with a brush or paint stick by dabbing or rubbing in a circular motion. Be careful not to push color under the edges of the stencil. Carefully remove the stencil after applying the color, then clean and dry it before reusing it (figure 11).

You can also make stencil resists by laying paper cutouts, leaves, tape, and found objects on the paper, applying color over them, and then removing the objects, which creates negative shapes. Spraying or spattering paint is the best application method, since the objects (except the tape) are loose.

tie-dyeing

This technique works best with papers that are strong enough to withstand soaking in a dye bath, such as Japanese papers. You can use many types of dyes, including Procion fiber-reactive dyes, which are available from weaving suppliers; Rit dyes, available at craft stores; vegetable dyes that can be made from natural sources, such as onion skins or walnut shells; and thinned acrylic paint. Prepare a dye bath following the instructions on the dye's label. Exercise caution when using chemical dyes—wear a face mask and rubber gloves.

Crumple the paper and bundle little sections with rubber bands, just as you would to tie-dye a piece of cloth. Make sure the rubber bands are tight. Soak the paper in the dye bath for a few minutes until the paper turns the desired color. Lift the paper from the dye bath and rinse it thoroughly until the water runs clear. Remove the rubber bands, and rings of undyed areas created by the rubber bands will appear (figure 12). Hang or lay the paper out to dry. Iron it between sheets of newsprint to flatten it, if desired.

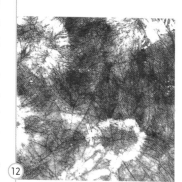

11

12

adding texture
and dimension

There are many interesting ways to add dimensional beauty to paper. Simple pleats can subtly enhance paper.

You can create more dramatic effects by sewing buttons onto a shade or screen or making pockets to hold interesting artifacts. A variety of embossed, crumpled, woven, and other dimensional papers are available in stores, or you can create your own textured paper with these simple techniques.

accordion pleats

Simple accordion-folded pleats are interesting in themselves, but you can also cut pop-ups out of the pleats or run folded paper through a sewing machine, creating a pierced design. To get the most accurate pleats, first fold your paper in half, then in quarters (figure 1), then in eighths (figure 2), and so on. Some folds will then need to be reversed so that they fold in the right direction and create the accordion.

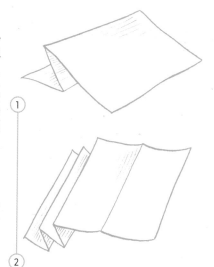

collaging textured items

Glue, sew, or embed textured items, such as buttons, leaves, or fabric, onto a sheet of paper. Check out sewing stores for interesting sequins, beads, and trims.

crumpling

There is a Japanese paper called *momigami,* which is literally crumpled into a ball after it is made, allowed to dry, and then flattened, resulting in an all-over crinkled texture (figure 3). You can purchase this paper or make it yourself.

embossing

Create raised images or patterns on your paper with embossing stencils available from craft stores. Or make your own stencils by drawing, tracing, or photocopying a simple design onto a piece of card stock, Bristol board, or lightweight mat board. Use positive or negative images (note that negative images will appear in reverse, so you should emboss things that you read in reverse). Thin, found objects, such as plastic stencils, also make good embossing designs.

Glue the item you want to emboss onto a piece of Bristol board or card stock. Tape the paper to be embossed (a soft-rag or handmade paper works well) in the desired position over the cutout design. It is best to emboss on a light table or a window, so that you can see through the paper. Press into the area around the cutout with your finger first, and then use a bone folder or a ball-tipped burnisher (available at craft stores) to work around the edges of the cutout. Press gently to avoid tearing the paper (figure 4, paper by Zelda Tanenbaum).

origami

The Japanese art of paper folding is something almost everyone has tried in school. Artists are constantly working on new ways to fold paper. Chris Palmer showed me his unique design (figure 5), which is beautiful when held up to the light. He used glassine paper, which is thin, translucent, and very easy to fold.

paper pockets

Sew or glue pockets onto a piece of paper and place items in the pockets to add a decorative effect. Vary the shapes and sizes of the pockets. Use deckle-edge scissors to create unique edges. This technique is used in the Pocket Shade project (see pages 52–55).

patchwork

Need a project for all of those paper scraps you've accumulated? Use a sewing machine to stitch small sheets of paper together to create a larger patchwork piece (figure 6, paper by Jennifer Morrow Wilson). The holes created by the needle will allow light to pass through when the paper is illuminated.

4

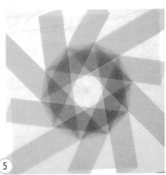

5

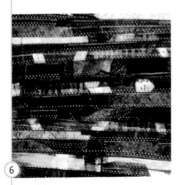

6

pop-ups

Cut slits in paper to create windows or flaps that reveal light or another paper beneath, or try something more complex and create paper structures with origami. There are some interesting how-to books available on origamic architecture (see Recommended Reading). Instructions for one type of pop-up (figure 7) can be found on pages 24–27.

weaving

Although this technique may look complicated, it is really quite simple. Create a warp and a weft from various papers and weave the sheets together (figure 8). Refer to the diagram (figure 9) to get started with simple patterns, and then experiment to create your own warps and wefts.

Homage to Innis, by Ruth Timm, of western Massachusetts, is a handmade paper scroll (18 in. x 58 in. per panel) inspired by the artist's interest in basketry. Timm made the sheets of paper and then adhered colored fibers while they were wet to build the images. After the paper dried, she cut strips into the paper to create a warp, and then she wove in strips of paper in similar hues. The artist came up with the clever idea of hanging loops of paper on a rod after becoming frustrated that the subtle texture of the handmade paper was lost when it was mounted under glass.
Photo by Bob Frechette.

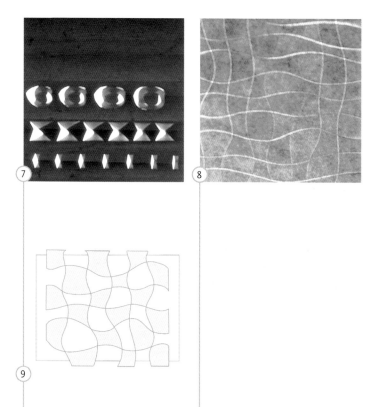

7

8

9

paper and candlelight

As a child I spent many winters in northern New Mexico, where candlelight made a big impression on me. During the holidays, driveways and rooftops were lined with brown paper bags, which were weighted down with sand and candles. The soft glow of the candle made the otherwise dull paper come to life.

There is something magical about the flicker of candlelight. Surrounding it with paper adds another dimension, softening the glow and providing something beautiful to look at. Since candles are small and self-contained, it is easy to construct lanterns to fit around them.

Always exercise caution when using candles. Put them in votive holders and make sure that the flame can't reach the paper or anything else and that they are safe from pets and small children. Never leave burning candles unattended.

pop-up lantern

Candles are a natural centerpiece for a tabletop. Why not add another dimension by covering your candle with this beautiful shade? A piece of translucent vellum paper softens the candlelight and keeps it from glaring through the holes in the pop-ups.

I got hooked on making pop-up architectural sculpture while taking an art class in Germany and was further inspired by books on origamic architecture. What is really fascinating about pop-ups is that a single, flat sheet of paper can be manipulated into a three-dimensional object merely by cutting and folding. When it is reflattened, the paper returns to its original, two-dimensional state.

selecting the paper

Use a lightweight card stock that folds well. Make sure the grain is running parallel to the folds. The paper can be opaque or translucent, since the light will shine through the pop-ups regardless of the transparency.

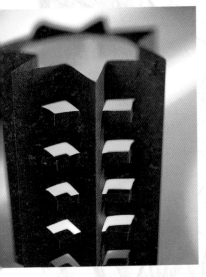

materials

- Lightweight card stock, 20¼ x 6 inches (grain should be in the 6-inch direction)
- Ruler
- Card stock, 1¼ x 6 inches
- Cutting mat
- Bone folder
- White glue or ¼-inch double-sided tape
- Heavy vellum, 8⅝ x 5¾ inches
- Glass votive candleholder
- Tea light or votive candle

folding the accordion

1. Lay the lightweight card stock on the work surface and use the ruler to place a mark ¼ inch in from one of the short ends. Make the first fold up to that mark. This extra ¼ inch will become the seam.

2. Follow the accordion fold diagram (see page 19) and accordion fold the paper until the pleats are 1¼ inches, starting at one end and making the first fold so that it meets the fold of the ¼-inch seam.

making a cutting template and cutting the pop-ups

1. Create a cutting template with the small piece of card stock using the diagram (figure 1) as a guide (see page 128 for a larger pattern). Use a craft knife or scissors to remove the tabs.

6"

1¼"

①

2. Working on a cutting mat, start at the side opposite the ¼-inch fold. Unfold the first pleat on the accordion-folded paper and lay it on the work surface. Place the template on that first panel with the edge of cut notches at the fold. Carefully draw and then cut the slits (figure 2). Make only the vertical slits—do not make any horizontal slits, as you did when making the template.

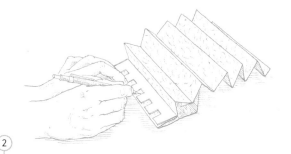

3. Place a ruler or straight edge at the bottom edge of the slits to keep them aligned. Use a bone folder to carefully make score marks between the cuts, which will make the tabs easier to fold.

4. Repeat steps 2 and 3 on all of the folded sections.

folding the pop-ups

1. Starting with the first pleat, take one scored section and fold it over, creasing along the scored line. Fold it in one direction and then bend it backward and crease it in the other direction (figure 3).

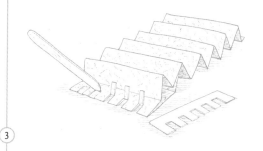

2. Continue creasing the other sections in the pleat.

3. Open the entire pleat and push the creased sections through the fold so that they pop up (figure 4).

4. Repeat steps 1 through 3 on every pleat.

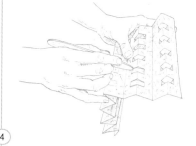

final assembly

1. With the pop-ups showing as mountain folds (popping out to look like peaks), apply white glue or a piece of double-sided tape to the ¼-inch seam and attach it to the edge of the pleat on the opposite side (figure 5).

2. Apply a piece of double-sided tape to one of the shorter edges of the vellum. Attach the edge to the opposite side to create a cylinder.

3. Place the cylinder inside of the star lantern and place them both over the glass votive candleholder. Place the tea light or the votive candle inside the votive holder.

shadow
lantern

In the 1640s, a German priest living in Rome developed the Magic Lantern, which cast shadows from glass

slides onto a screen, a precursor to modern cinema. This shadow lantern works on the same principle. A light source inside casts the shadow from a stencil onto a paper screen.

This little lantern is fun to make as an embellishment for your mantel, windowsill, or kitchen table. The instructions make a lantern that is 4½ inches wide and 6 inches tall. You can alter the dimensions as you please, but keep in mind that 4½ inches is the minimum width for candle use. Also, if your lantern gets much larger, you should switch to a stronger wood, such as pine, and joint the wood at the corners. You may also need to make crossbars in the middle, similar to those used in the Japanese-style screen (see page 63).

selecting the paper

The stencil paper for this project should be a card-weight stock that can be cut with a craft knife. The screen paper should be semi-translucent, so that the shadow cast by the candle inside will be visible.

materials

- Carbon paper or photocopy machine
- Small piece of card stock
- Craft knife
- Stencil paper: 4 pieces of 4½- x 6-inch card stock
- Cutting mat
- Straight edge
- Screen paper: 4 pieces of 5½ x 7-inch semi-translucent paper
- 8 pieces of ¼-inch-square strips of balsa wood, cut to 4 inches in length
- 8 pieces of ¼-inch-square strips of balsa wood, 6 inches in length
- Small saw (a Japanese or jeweler's saw works well)
- Sandpaper
- White glue
- Acrylic paint (optional)
- Hinge strips: 4 strips of 6- x ½-inch paper (to make a lantern) OR 3 strips of 6- x ¾-inch paper (to make a screen), cut out of either the matching screen paper or another strong, thin paper

making a stencil design

1. To start this project, you will need to design a pattern. Textile designs, tile patterns, and architectural details are great sources of inspiration. There are many copyright-free clip-art books full of interesting designs and patterns. Of course, you can work freehand and just draw your own design.

2. Once you choose a design, trace it or use a photocopy machine to enlarge, reduce, or repeat patterns to create a 3½-inch by 5½-inch image area (your pattern should have at least a solid ¼-inch border all around). The cutouts should be at least ¼ inch in width in order to cast a shadow when the lantern is illuminated.

making a pattern

1. Your lantern can have the same design on all four sides, or you can create four different patterns. If you use the same design on all four sides, it is useful to create a pattern. Make the pattern 4½ inches by 6 inches—the same size that your finished panels will be.

2. Using carbon paper, trace the design onto a piece of card stock (you can also photocopy the design directly onto the card stock, if you prefer). Use a craft knife to cut out the pattern.

3. Trace the pattern(s) onto the four stencil panels. Working on a cutting mat and using a straight edge and a craft knife, cut out the design (figure 1). Depending on the thickness of the card stock, you may be able to layer two or more pieces and cut them at the same time.

creating the panels

1. Start with one stencil panel (card stock with cutouts) and two 4-inch and two 6-inch lengths of balsa wood. *Note:* Most balsa wood has the printing or paint on the ends for retail sales purposes. These features may show in your final product, so I recommend either cutting them off with a small saw or using sandpaper to remove them.

2. Apply glue to one side of a 6-inch strip of balsa wood and place it glue-side down onto one edge of the stencil (figure 2). (If there are pencil marks on your stencil, glue the balsa wood to that side—the marks will not be visible on the final piece.)

3. Glue the other three strips of balsa wood to the outer edges of the stencil panel. I don't apply glue to the corner joints of the wood on lanterns this small. Repeat steps 1 through 3 to make the other three panels.

gluing tip

Always put adhesive on the object you are gluing. Apply adhesive to the entire surface and, if it is a piece of paper, glue "out" onto a piece of scrap paper so that you spread the glue all the way to the very edges (see below). Keep a damp paper towel nearby to clean off your fingers, since they may get a little sticky. This will keep excess glue from getting on the surface of your materials.

1

2

amanda degener

Amanda Degener created *Winter* from sheets of paper made from the inner bark of Kozo and Gampi fibers. She feels that there is a luminous quality to this Asian-style paper that seems to capture the soul of nature. Degener believes that she, too, has inner fiber, which, when illuminated, provides her soul with nutrients.

Her icon has always been the tree, because it unites the earth and sky. She hopes her artwork visually nourishes and helps her and others see and feel the ground as well as the heavens. Degener finds beauty in the subtle palette of this piece, as the colors reflect her experience of nature during the long winters in her home of Minneapolis, Minnesota. *Photo by Amanda Degener.*

attaching the screen paper

1. Use the template (figure 3) as a guide to cut out the four screen papers. Be sure to cut the small slits at each corner (see page 128 for a larger pattern).

2. Set a piece of screen paper face down on your work surface. Place one of the assembled panels with balsa wood stencil-side down and apply glue to the edges of the balsa wood that are facing up.

3. Carefully lift the panel and set it on top of the screen paper, glue-side down, centering the panel on the sheet, making sure the corners line up with the inside ends of the slits (figure 4). Flip the entire panel over (with the screen paper attached) and rub your fingers over the glued paper, smoothing out any wrinkles.

4. Turn the panel back over and apply glue to the excess paper on one of the short sides. Fold it up and over the balsa wood, neatly covering the side and top edges (figure 5). Fold the two small tabs over onto the adjacent sides of the panel. Repeat this step on the opposite short side.

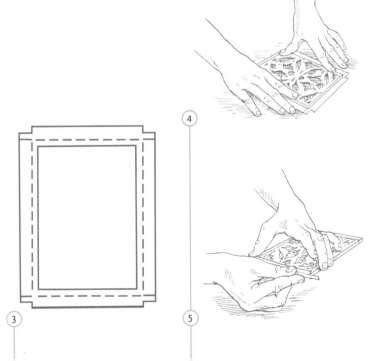

3

4

5

5. Apply glue to the excess paper on one of the long sides and wrap the paper over the side and top edges of the balsa wood, covering the tabs. Repeat this step on the other long side.

6. Repeat steps 1 through 5 to create the other three panels.

making hinges for a lantern

Follow these instructions if you wish to make a lantern. If you prefer to make a folding screen, skip to Variation: Making a Screen at the end of these directions.

materials
- 4 strips of 6- x ¾-inch paper, cut from matching screen paper
- Bone folder
- Straight edge
- White glue
- Glue brush
- Scrap paper

1. Make a pattern for the hinges (figure 6) and use it to cut four hinges out of the same paper that you used for the screen paper, or use another strong and flexible paper (see page 128 for a larger pattern).

2. Score the hinges lengthwise and fold them in half.

time-saving variation

If you don't want to wrap the sides of the lantern panels with paper, you can use an acrylic paint that matches or complements the screen paper and paint the edges of the balsa wood strips. You'll need to paint them before you attach them to the stenciled paper, but you need to paint only one side, since the other sides will not be seen. It is easy to lay several strips together and paint them all at one time. Then, simply cut the screen paper to 4½ inches by 6 inches and glue it to the other side of the balsa wood panel. For this version, apply a light weight, such as a book, for a few minutes to allow the glue to set.

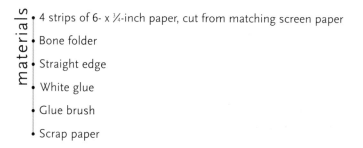

6

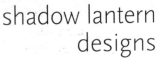

shadow lantern designs

You can vary the number of panels to create a triangular, pentagonal, or hexagonal lantern. You can also vary the shape of the panels. Since a screen is visible on both sides, you can also put the stencil on the front of the screen to accentuate the design rather than the shadow.

3. Lay two lantern panels side by side with the stencil side facing up. Use a straight edge to make sure the bottom edges all line up. Unfold one hinge strip, apply glue to one side, and lay it over the two sections with the fold in the center of the two panels (figure 7). Hold it in place for a moment to set. Fold the two panels along the hinge and check its position, making sure it is firmly in place.

4. Unfold the two panels and place them face down on your work surface. Place another panel next to the set. Repeat step 3 to hinge the third panel to the second one, and then the fourth to the third.

5. When gluing the final hinge to complete the lantern, attach half of the hinge strip to one edge of the lantern (figure 8).

6. Carefully apply glue to the unattached edge of the hinge strip (take care not to get glue on any other part of the lantern) and fold the other unattached panel onto the strip, applying pressure to make sure that the hinge sticks to the final panel.

variation: making a screen

1. If you prefer to make a folding screen instead of a lantern, you have two options. You can use the same hinges for the lantern (see Making Hinges for a Lantern, page 33) and apply every other one to the opposite sides of the panels, so that the panels unfold like an accordion. Or you can create the double-jointed hinges described in the Japanese-style screen project (see Making Hinges for a Screen, page 66), which allow the panels to flex in both directions. In either case, do not attach the end panels to each other so that the screen can remain open and can be viewed from both sides.

isamu noguchi

In 1951, Isamu Noguchi visited Gifu Prefecture, where cormorant fishing in the Nagara River was a famed event.

Inspired by the candle-lit lanterns that illuminated the fishing on the river at night, Noguchi sketched what was to become his trademark—the Akari lamp, which means "light as illumination." Gifu, a major center for the pro-duction of mulberry-bark paper and bamboo umbrellas, also produced more than half of the paper lanterns in Japan. The mayor asked Noguchi to help revive the city's paper lantern industry by creating new lamps for the American and European markets.

Noguchi used traditional and modern design to redesign the city's style of lanterns. He replaced the candle with a lightbulb and kept the traditional bamboo strips, adding an internal metal armature that allowed the lamps to assume a variety of sculptural forms without obtrusive frames. Noguchi also developed three- and four-legged bases, above which the light sculptures seemed to float. He wound thin strips of bamboo in a spiral around multi-part wooden molds that defined the overall shape of the end products. Then he glued strips of Mino paper onto the bamboo structures. Once they were dry, he disassembled and removed the internal molds. The manufacturer was then able to collapse the paper forms so they could be packed into a flat box for shipping.

Noguchi's spirit lives on in the more than one hundred Akari forms produced today. Noguchi viewed his lanterns as physical expressions of metaphysical concepts, their essence as light in the sense of weightlessness. Their very nature, he once said, "questions materiality, and is consonant with our appreciation today of the less thingness of things, the less encumbered perceptions." *Photo from the Isamu Noguchi Museum in Long Island City, New York.*

votive
cover

Light up the outdoors with these festive votive candles, which can be strung along a porch or hung from the branches of trees, much like a string of electric holiday lights. The candles in these mini lanterns create a soft, glowing ambiance that is unmatched by electricity.

You can use brightly colored, translucent vellum paper to add another design element, as well. Try decorating with a variety of colors to create visual interest and a lively mood.

SAFETY NOTE: As with any candle, do not leave these lanterns unattended when lit.

selecting the paper

Bold, translucent papers work best for this project, since the candlelight provides a soft glow. Use paper that is stiff and has some body to it, so that the votive cover holds its shape.

materials

FOR ONE VOTIVE COVER

- 20-gauge wire, 24 inches long
- Glass votive holders, 2½ inches in diameter
- Needle-nosed pliers
- Paper, 8 x 3½ inches
- Ruler
- Triangle
- X-acto knife
- Bone folder
- ¼- or ½-inch double-sided tape
- Votive candle or tea light

twisting the wire hanger

1. Wrap the wire around the glass votive holder just below the middle and twist it a couple of times (figure 1).

2. Pull the wire underneath the bottom of the glass and over to the other side, threading it through the circumference wire. Remove the glass and wrap the wire around the circumference wire a couple of times. Pinch it tight with pliers.

3. Bring the loose end of the wire around to meet the original twisted joint and twist the end of the loose wire around to the left and right of the original joint to hold it in place.

4. Place the glass in the wire holder. Pinch the top loop together with needle-nosed pliers and twist the wire 3 times.

5. Bend the top to create a hook.

1

making the paper shade

1. Place the piece of paper face down on your work surface. With a ruler, draw two lines along the 8-inch length of the strip, ½ inch in from each edge.

2. Using a triangle, draw slits perpendicular to and between the two lines at ½-inch intervals. Cut the slits with an X-acto knife (figure 2).

3. Use a bone folder to score the paper along the two horizontal lines. Make a third crease with the bone folder in the center of the length of the strip. Carefully erase any pencil marks.

4. Fold the strip of paper in half, with the right side facing out. Fold the strip in the other direction along the other two scored lines (figure 3).

5. Apply a strip of double-sided tape to one of the short edges on the wrong side and wrap the paper strip around the glass votive. Attach the taped edge to the other short edge (the right side) to complete the miniature lantern. Place the candle in the votive holder.

éatrice coron

Four paper-cut cards slip into the sides of this wooden lamp (which measures 6 in. x 6 in. x 10 in.) made by artist Béatrice Coron of New York City. Coron creates one-of-a-kind and editioned books, illustrations, and prints, all with her exquisite paper cuts. *Photo by Béatrice Coron.*

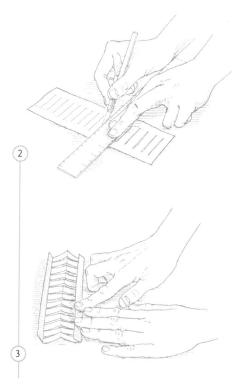

paper and natural light

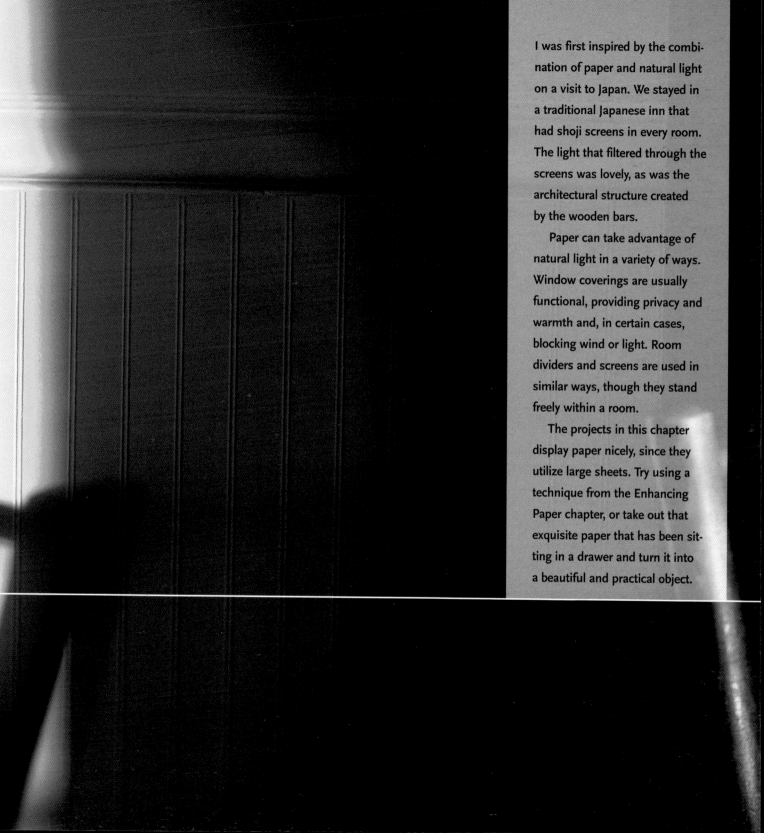

I was first inspired by the combination of paper and natural light on a visit to Japan. We stayed in a traditional Japanese inn that had shoji screens in every room. The light that filtered through the screens was lovely, as was the architectural structure created by the wooden bars.

Paper can take advantage of natural light in a variety of ways. Window coverings are usually functional, providing privacy and warmth and, in certain cases, blocking wind or light. Room dividers and screens are used in similar ways, though they stand freely within a room.

The projects in this chapter display paper nicely, since they utilize large sheets. Try using a technique from the Enhancing Paper chapter, or take out that exquisite paper that has been sitting in a drawer and turn it into a beautiful and practical object.

horizontal
accordion blind

What better way to display a beautiful sheet of paper than to hang it in front of a window, so that it can be illuminated naturally? You can easily find a variety of decorative papers in large sizes (some even come in rolls), which makes them perfect for large windows. If the sheets aren't quite big enough, join them in an interesting way, such as with a collage decoration or by sewing them together. The Enhancing Paper chapter should give you plenty of ideas.

This horizontally pleated pull-blind opens with a draw cord and can cover an entire window. You have two mounting options with this shade: You can mount it within the frame of the window or hang it in front of the window. You should choose the mounting option you prefer before making the shade.

selecting the paper

Use a strong, light cover-weight paper that will maintain its shape and hold up to opening and closing. I like elephant hide (sometimes called marbled parchment), which is available at art-supply stores. It is very important that the grain of the paper follows the direction of the pleats.

materials

- Tape measure
- Shade paper
- Calculator
- Bone folder
- Hole punch (the type of punch will depend on the width of the pleats; a stationer's punch will work for some shades, but others may require a hole punch with a deeper reach)
- Clear plastic hole reinforcers
- Drill and bits
- 2 strips of wood lathe or basswood with a depth of ¼ inch or slightly less and a width of one pleat or slightly less, cut to the length of the pleats
- White glue
- Paint or stain (optional)
- Cord, ⅛ inch in diameter and 5 times the length of the window opening

determining the size of the blind

1. Measure the inside dimensions of the window opening with a tape measure.

2. Determine the shade's width, which depends on how it will be mounted (see page 43). If it will be mounted within the window frame, cut the shade paper to the width of the window minus 1 inch. If it will be mounted in front of the window frame, cut the shade paper to the width of the window plus 2 inches. For example, the width of my window opening is 35 inches, so I subtracted 1 inch and cut the shade to be 34 inches wide.

3. Determine the shade's length. The length should be 50 percent longer than the height of the window opening to accommodate the accordions. It may be necessary to join a couple of pieces of paper together. For example, the height of my window opening is 50 inches. 50 inches x 50% = 25 inches, and 50 + 25 gives me a total paper length of 75 inches.

making the shade

1. Using a bone folder, fold the paper accordion-style using the technique described on page 19. It is especially important to use this technique with large sheets of paper; otherwise, the pleats will not be neat and uniform. Keep folding until the pleat size is between 1 and 2 inches (this will vary according to the size of the original sheet of paper).

2. Punch the holes for the draw cord. Starting with the pleat that is second from the top, make a mark 6 inches in from the left side and 6 inches in from the right side. Be careful to center all of the holes within the width of the pleat. Find the center of the pleat length and punch a hole 4 inches in both directions from the center.

3. Hold two or three pleats beneath the holes punched in step 2 and use those holes as a guide to punch through the pleats below (figure 1). Unfold the paper and use the bottom-most pleat with holes to be your guide for punching a few more pleats beneath it. Continue punching until you reach the second-from-the-last pleat.

4. Apply hole reinforcers to both sides of the holes for the best support.

5. Drill holes in the two pieces of wood lathe to line up with the holes on the pleats of the shade. Glue the strips of wood to the top and bottom paper panels (figure 2). I like seeing the wood as an accent on my shade, but you could paint, stain, or cover it with paper prior to gluing it to the shade.

6. Thread the cord through the holes in the shade and the wood (figure 3).

mounting the shade: option 1

This option allows you to mount the shade to the inside of the window frame so that it fits into the window recess and lies flush with the wall on both sides.

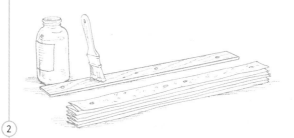

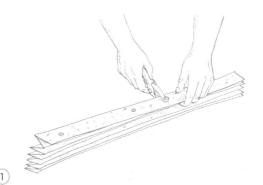

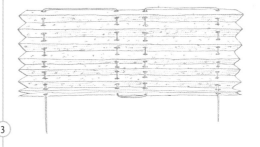

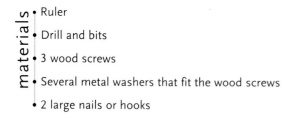

materials
- Ruler
- Drill and bits
- 3 wood screws
- Several metal washers that fit the wood screws
- 2 large nails or hooks

joining two sheets of paper

If the shade needs to be longer than one sheet of paper will allow, I recommend gluing over an entire accordion pleat, which means that the paper will be doubled on that pleat. This double thickness may be more noticeable in some papers than in others. If it is noticeable, try using a decorative effect to make it more interesting. For instance, leave the pleat you are gluing onto intact, but cut the other one with deckle-edge scissors or in a wave or zigzag pattern, or punch holes in it to add interest when it is illuminated.

Some windows are wider than standard papers. If you need to add width to the paper, I recommend making a series of mini-shades that can be drawn up separately rather than gluing two sheets of paper together.

1. With a ruler, make three marks on the top piece of the wooden lathe: one 2 inches in from both ends and one in the very center. Make sure the marks are centered vertically in the wood. Drill a hole at each mark.

2. Mark these same points on the inside top of the window frame and drill pilot holes with a smaller drill bit.

3. Since the cord runs over the top of the wooden lathe, there must be some space between the top of the shade and the window frame. Therefore, put a few washers in between the wooden lathe and the screws before you mount the shade to the window frame (figure 4).

4. Drill the screws into the wood lathe and window frame.

5. Install nails or hooks around which you can wrap the cord when the blind is open.

mounting the shade: option 2

This option allows you to mount the shade to the wall just above the window so that it hangs in front of the window.

materials
- Ruler
- 3 angle irons with short wood screws to attach to the wood lathe and ¼-inch wood screws to attach to the wall
- Drill and bits
- Level
- 2 large nails or hooks

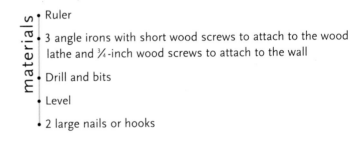

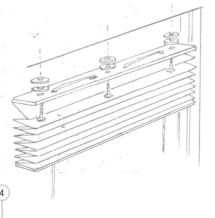

4

1. Using the ruler, make three marks on the top piece of the wooden lathe: one mark 2 inches in from both ends and one in the very center. Make sure the marks are centered vertically in the wood. Place an angle iron at each mark and mark the screw holes. Drill holes at each point.

2. Attach the three angle irons to the wooden lathe with the short screws.

3. Set the wooden lathe in place above the window frame and mark where the angles will be mounted (use a level to make sure the blind hangs straight). Drill pilot holes in the wall.

4. Mount the blind to the wall with the ¾-inch wood screws (figure 5).

5. Install nails or hooks around which you can wrap the cord when the blind is open.

operating the paper blind

To close the blind, pull down on the center loop of the cord (figure 6). To open the blind, pull down and out to the sides on the two loose ends of the cord (figure 7).

oko ibe

Asuka, an installation at the Sendai Building in Japan (13m x 13m x 32m), was made by Kyoko Ibe, of Kyoto, Japan. In Japan, where Ibe was educated, handmade paper is used both for all types of practical purposes, and as surfaces on which to create art. Ibe was inspired to use the medium as the art form in and of itself. Some of her installations are monumental in scale. She often invites wind and light to come into her work, which draw attention to the paper and create a catalyst between people and space. *Photo by Kyoko Ibe.*

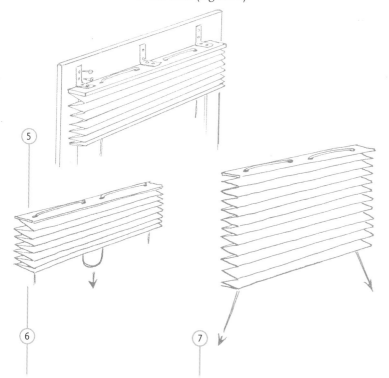

5

6

7

vertical
accordion blind

Pleating is something unique that you can do with the right paper. I enjoy running the pleats through a sewing machine to make pierced holes for light to shine through. There are other options that work well for pleats, such as pop-ups, so I hope you will take this project to new dimensions.

This window shade is simple and fun to make. It can be used as a full shade for small windows or as a half-shade for a large window. Magnets or clips hold it open and closed. It can hang on a U-shaped curtain rod or on a straight rod with hooks, but I think it works best when it's hung on a curtain rod mounted within the window frame.

selecting the paper

Use a cover-weight paper that folds well and maintains its shape. Make sure that the grain follows the direction of the pleats.

materials

- Ruler
- Bone folder
- 2 sheets shade paper (3 if the window is very wide)
- Sewing machine (optional)
- Card stock
- Grommet punch
- ½-inch grommets in silver or gold
- Hammer
- Double-sided tape (optional, needed with circular magnets)
- ½-inch circular magnets or other craft magnets (optional)
- Spray paint (optional)
- 18 metal or plastic curtain rings that fit through the grommets
- Curtain rod

making the shade

1. Using the ruler, measure the inside dimensions of the window opening. I made my shade to cover the bottom half of a window, and the directions that follow reflect that. My paper is 30 inches wide and 28 inches high, with the grain running in the 28-inch direction.

2. Use the bone folder to accordion fold each sheet of paper with the grain until the pleats are between 1 and 2 inches wide. This will vary depending on the original paper size (see the folding directions on page 19).

3. This step is optional. Run each folded pleat one at a time through an unthreaded sewing machine to create a pierced pattern (figure 1). I used the widest zigzag stitch and moved the paper to the left and right as I stitched down the pleat to create a line that curved back and forth.

4. Make a template for punching the grommet holes. Cut a piece of card stock into a square that measures the width of one pleat. Punch a hole in the center of the square.

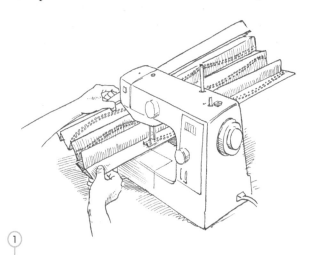

①

5. Place the template at the top of the first left-hand pleat and use it as a guide for punching a hole. Punch the left side of every pleat and the final pleat on the right side. Repeat this step for each sheet of folded shade paper.

6. Slip the male part of the grommet into the punched hole from underneath and set the grommet punch beneath it. Set the female part of the grommet on top of the paper. Place the top of the grommet punch on top of that, and pound it a couple of times with a hammer to join the two pieces. Repeat this step until all of the grommets are installed (figure 2).

7. Repeat steps 2 through 6 with the other paper panel(s).

attaching the magnets

1. Lay the paper panels on the work surface in the position in which they will be hung in the window.

2. Apply double-sided tape to the back of 7 magnets (this number may vary with the height of the paper shade—use one magnet every 4 inches). Attach the magnets to the inside panel, centering them widthwise and spacing them approximately 4 inches apart (figure 3). You may need to measure and mark the locations before attaching the magnets, if necessary.

3. Place another magnet on top of each of the magnets that you just affixed to the panel, making sure that they do not repel one another. Apply double-sided tape to the sides of the magnets that are not joined to the other magnets. A double set of magnets should be visible with the adhesive showing on only one set.

4. Carefully take the second panel of paper and align the middle strip with the strip holding the magnets. Press in place to adhere the magnets to that strip.

5. Spray paint the curtain rings to match the grommets, if desired. Attach the curtain rings to the shade, mount the curtain rod, and hang the shade.

creating a paper mosaic

Here's another idea for a window covering. This is a really simple project; the only hard part is coming up with a design! This project works well on interior windows, doors with windows, bathroom windows, or any window where you want to create privacy yet allow light to pass through. This shade is semi-permanent, meaning you can't open and close it, but you can remove it entirely if you want to change your window treatment.

Measure the window panels and start with a piece of paper that size. Create a design that has spaces between shapes. Transfer the design to a sheet of paper and cut out the shapes. Attach the pieces to the window with Velcro, magnets, spray glue, or double-sided tape.

pocket
shade

I've always loved pockets—clothing with lots of pockets, jackets with hidden pockets, handbags with pockets in which to tuck things away. So when I saw pocket shades made of fabric, the wheels in my brain started churning. Although I enjoy sewing, using tape instead of thread is a lot easier.

This paper pocket shade can hang in a window, but it isn't really meant to block light or add privacy. It is a decorative object, with pockets for displaying items, such as feathers, leaves, or photographs.

You can display a collection in a unique way and even remove and rearrange the items whenever you wish. There are lots of possibilities and lots of variations. Try making the pockets out of different papers or varying the pocket shapes and sizes.

selecting the paper

I recommend using a soft, translucent paper because it filters light well. The pockets can be made of the same paper as the shade or of other papers to create an interesting design.

materials

- 2 sheets paper, 25 x 37 inches
- Yardstick
- Triangle
- Straight edge
- Craft knife
- Cutting mat
- ¼-inch double-sided tape
- Something to hang the shade on, such as a curtain rod, piece of bamboo, or copper tubing

creating the hanging tabs

1. Place the sheet of paper on your work surface and trim ¼ inch off the long edge so that the sheet measures 24¾ x 37 inches. (This measurement is arbitrary. I wanted my tabs to be approximately 2 inches wide. When I did the math, there was an extra ¼ inch of paper, which I decided to remove.)

2. Using the yardstick, measure and lightly draw a parallel line 4 inches from the top edge.

3. Use the triangle and a straight edge to draw lines perpendicular to the first line at 2¼-inch intervals to create the hanging tabs. You can cut these with a craft knife and a cutting mat without drawing guidelines, if you desire. Cut along all of the lines and then remove every other section by cutting along the 4-inch line, starting one tab in from the end, and ending one tab in from the other end (figure 1).

4. Apply double-sided tape to the top edge of every other tab and fold the tabs in half, attaching the tape to the drawn line to create the paper loops. You should end up with six tabs (this will depend on your paper size).

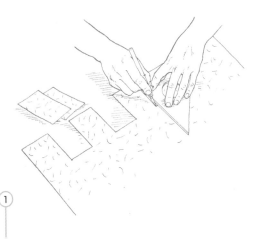

1

making the pockets

1. From the second sheet of paper, cut nine pockets measuring 5 inches in width and 7⅛ inches in length.

2. Apply double-sided tape to both of the 7⅛-inch sides and one of the 5-inch sides (figure 2). The taped 5-inch side is the bottom of the pocket.

3. Follow the diagram to create the spacing of the pockets on the shade (figure 3).

4. Remove the protective backing on the tape, pocket by pocket, and adhere the pockets to the shade. Use a straight edge and a triangle as you attach the pockets to make sure they are straight (figure 4).

5. Insert the tabs into a curtain rod (bamboo, dowel, and copper tubing are inexpensive alternatives) and hang your shade. Place flat objects, such as feathers, leaves, and paper shapes, into the pockets.

In creating *Butterfly Twig* (approx. 10 ft. x 12 ft. x 6 ft.), Ming Fay, of New York City, used large circular leaves similar to those on the Chinese money tree. His artwork is suspended in a sun-filled atrium; air currents and human movement cause the leaves to flutter as if they were in an exterior natural setting. Fay's piece suggests that people choose to surround themselves with nature, even if it is an artificial replication. *Photo by Ming Fay.*

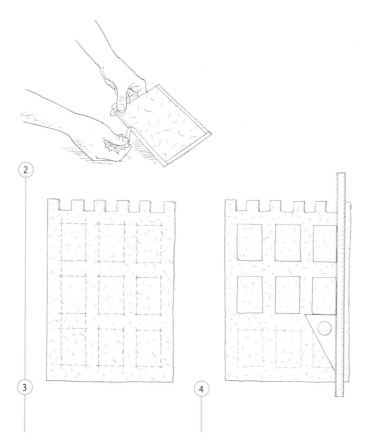

room
divider

Room dividers can hide a cluttered desk or separate areas in a room, and they can either block light or let light through, depending on the type of paper that is used. You can create room dividers from any number of panels depending on your needs, and the individual panel dimensions can vary as well.

Canvas stretcher bars are used to make the frame for this project. They can be purchased at art supply stores in almost any length. I recommend applying some sort of finish—I used linseed oil to seal my wood—but you can paint, stain, or decoupage the wood to enhance it and make it more interesting.

selecting the paper

Almost any paper will work, but I recommend using a paper that will not shrink when it's wet, particularly if your screen is large. The paper will expand a bit when it's glued, and it may expand and contract with humidity changes, causing the paper to rip or pull away from the wood frame.

materials

- 4 canvas stretcher bars, 1½ inches wide and 58 inches long
- 4 canvas stretcher bars, 1½ inches wide and 17 inches long
- Wood glue
- Glue brush
- Linseed oil
- Paintbrush or foam brush
- Yardstick
- 3 hinges, ⅝ inches long
- Drill
- ⁷⁄₆₄-inch drill bit
- Screwdriver or screwdriver drill bit
- Rice paste (see recipe on page 59)
- Paper, 57⅜ x 16⅜ inches (I cut my paper slightly larger and trimmed it to this final size just prior to gluing it)

Panel design by Jenny Pinto

designing the details

1. Think about whether light should filter through the screen or not. I used a fairly translucent paper and layered another paper on top of it to create an image. In addition, I had to use two pieces of paper per panel, since a single sheet of paper was not long enough. I incorporated matching tears and left a small space between the two sheets as part of the design.

making the frames

1. Put the stretcher bars' prejointed ends together with a bit of wood glue and a glue brush to create the rectangular wooden frames. The 17-inch stretcher bars will form the horizontal sides of the frame, and the 58-inch stretcher bars will form the vertical sides of the frame. Apply linseed oil to the wood with a paintbrush or foam brush.

2. Using the yardstick, measure and mark the placement of the hinges. One hinge should be approximately 8 inches from the top end, one hinge should be 8 inches from the bottom end, and one hinge should be in the center. *Note:* Canvas stretcher bars vary slightly in size. Measure everything from the bottom to ensure that the base of the screen is even and will sit on the floor properly.

I put the hinges on my panels prior to applying the paper, since my paper was fragile and I didn't want to risk poking a hole in it. If your paper is durable, you may opt to attach the paper first, particularly if you are assembling more than two panels. Most hinges bend only in one direction, so make sure that you attach them with the screens folding as you want them to. Otherwise, purchase reversible hinges, which fold in both directions, at a specialty hardware store.

3. Mark the screw holes with a pencil and predrill the holes with a drill bit that is smaller than the hinge screws. Attach the hinges (figure 1).

making rice paste

Rice paste is a traditional glue used for affixing paper to wood on Japanese-style screens (it is also used in bookbinding). It comes in powder form and must be cooked. Rice paste stays where it is applied, doesn't run, is invisible when dry, and is archival. However, it must be refrigerated and will not last longer than 4 to 6 days. It is nice to work with because it doesn't dry too quickly, allowing you time to shift and reposition the paper, if necessary. It is available at art supply stores and through bookbinding suppliers.

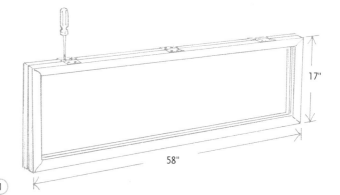

ingredients
- 3 cups water
- ¼ cup rice starch

1. Bring the water to a boil in a kettle.

2. Place ¼ cup of rice starch in a small, stainless steel saucepan. Add ½ cup of COLD water and whisk until smooth.

3. Cook the rice starch and water mixture over medium heat. Add ¼ cup of BOILING water from the kettle and continue to whisk until the mixture thickens and becomes translucent. The paste should not hold peaks, but if you place the whisk in the paste and then pull it out, it should leave a slight impression on the surface. If the glue is too thick, add a little water and mix well. If it is too thin, cook it longer, being careful not to burn it.

4. To cool the rice paste quickly so that you can work with it, partially submerge the saucepan in cold water and stir until the paste cools. If you don't stir it, a skin will form, which will later become blobs.

attaching the paper

1. Apply rice paste to the bottom edge of the frame, just inside the ridge, and attach the bottom edge of the paper, making sure that the rest of the sheet will fall into place (figure 2).

2. Roll the paper down toward the glued end. Apply more rice paste to both sides of the frame in 5-inch increments and unroll the paper, attaching it to the frame (figure 3).

3. Apply paste across the top of the wooden frame and attach the final paper edge.

4. Repeat steps 1 to 3 with the other panel(s).

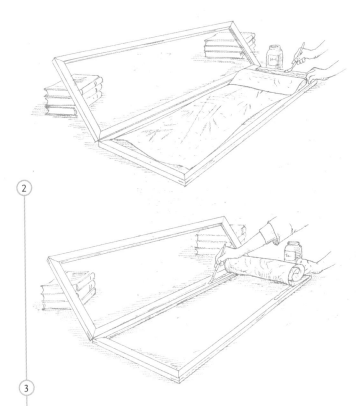

2

3

paul wong

This image-infused curtain was created by Paul Wong, of New York City. Wong xeroxed images onto translucent, handmade abaca paper to show the meager possessions of a Chinese peasant on one side and the abundant accouterments of an Emperor on the other. This comparison of class structure, which is based upon the ability to provide the dead with the necessary baggage to survive in the Chinese afterlife, suggests a social dichotomy that theoretically continues from real life into the spirit world. To Wong, the curtain is an intangible boundary defining these two places in the spirit world, thus the ethereal, membrane-like quality of the paper. *Photo by Paul Wong.*

Japanese-style
screen

Wood, paper, and other native materials are used in abundance in Japanese homes. *Shoji* screens serve as the principal partitioning device to provide privacy, in addition to furnishing a touch of exquisite illumination and decoration. In Japanese homes, shoji screens provide a boundary between indoors and out, allowing light through but keeping out drafts.

Shoji screens are made of thin wooden strips arranged in various rectangular patterns. The strips are notched to each other from alternate sides to give the frame strength. Usually, the paper is attached to the outside of the shoji screen so that the latticework can be seen from inside.

Traditional shoji screens require fine woodworking skills, which are a bit too complex for this book. Therefore, this Japanese-style screen is a simplified version made from balsa wood and bamboo barbecue skewers. You can also convert this screen into a lantern by attaching the ends of the screen to make a closed container.

selecting the paper

Any paper will work for this project. I prefer something translucent, which is enhanced by illumination. However, you can use a more opaque paper to block light. You can purchase traditional shoji screen paper at many art supply and fine paper stores.

materials

FOR ONE PANEL

- 2 pieces of ½ x ¼-inch balsa wood, cut to 8-inch lengths
- 2 pieces of ½ x ¼-inch balsa wood, cut to 10-inch lengths
- Craft knife or handsaw
- Fine sandpaper
- Ruler
- Drill
- ⁷⁄₆₄-inch drill bit
- Small piece of scrap wood
- 8 tacks
- Hammer
- 3 skewers, cut to 8½ inches
- 1 skewer, cut to 10 inches (some skewers are exactly 10 inches and won't need to be cut)
- Wood glue
- White glue
- Paper, cut to 8½ x 10 inches
- 4 pieces of strong Japanese tissue paper, cut to 1 x 2½ inches

preparing the balsa wood

These instructions are for making a four-paneled screen, so you'll need to quadruple the amounts in the materials list.

1. Balsa wood comes in 2- or 3-foot lengths and is very easy to cut, even with a craft knife or handsaw. I like to cut two pieces of wood at a time. Mark the two lengths of balsa wood with a pencil at an 8-inch and a 10-inch interval. Then cut the lengths and sand the ends so that they look neat and clean.

2. On one of the 8-inch lengths, measure and mark a hole for drilling at the center of the length (4 inches), ³⁄₁₆ inch in from the edge. Carefully drill the hole. When drilling through wood, always put a piece of scrap wood underneath. This provides support and prevents blowout on the back of the hole (figure 1).

3. Use the 8-inch piece of balsa wood with the hole as a template for drilling the other pieces. I drilled four pieces at a time. Place the predrilled length on top of three more lengths and line everything up. Carefully drill through the predrilled hole, making holes in the other pieces of balsa wood.

4. On one of the 10-inch lengths, measure and mark three holes for drilling at 2½, 5, and 7½ inches along the length of the wood and ³⁄₁₆ inch in from one edge. Carefully drill a hole at each point.

5. Use the 10-inch length with the holes as a template for drilling the other lengths. Place the predrilled length on top of three more lengths and line everything up. Carefully drill through the predrilled holes, making holes in the other lengths.

assembling the panel frames

1. To assemble one panel, arrange two 8-inch and two 10-inch lengths in a rectangle with the 10-inch pieces on the outside (the final width is 8½ inches). The ½-inch dimension of the wood is the depth of the panel. Make sure that the drilled holes in the 8-inch lengths match each other and that the drilled holes in the 10-inch lengths are opposite each other but line up (figure 2). Check the corners and sand down any ends that seem too long.

2. Starting with one corner, gently push a nail through one of the 10-inch lengths into the end of an 8-inch length, leaving room for a second nail (figure 3). Use a small hammer, if necessary. Push in a second nail to secure the joint.

3. Repeat step 2 on the other three corners.

4. Repeat steps 1 through 3 to assemble the other panel frames.

attaching the skewers

1. Cut the skewers to the proper length with the handsaw. For each panel there should be three skewers that measure 8½ inches and one that measures 10 inches.

2. Push the horizontal 8½-inch skewers through the holes to check their fit. Sand the ends, if necessary. Do the same with the 10-inch skewer (figure 4). If the skewers are loose in their holes, carefully apply a dab of wood glue to each end to hold them in place.

3. Repeat steps 1 and 2 on the remaining three panels.

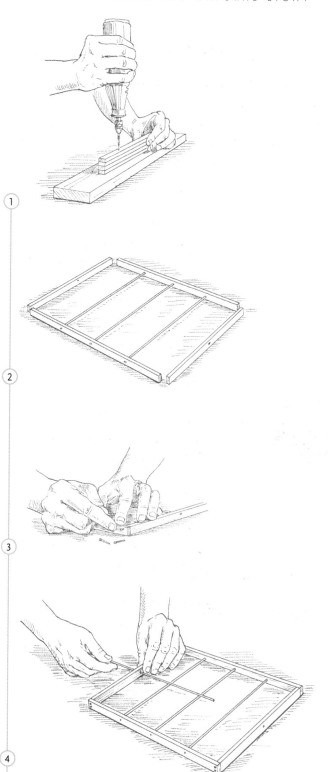

Alternative Design

5

applying the paper

1. Place one assembled balsa wood panel face down on your work surface with the vertical skewer closest to the table top and apply white glue to all four edges of the back of the wooden frame. Carefully set a piece of paper on top of the frame, lining up the edges as you lay it down and smoothing out any creases (figure 5). Turn the panel over and apply some weight, such as a couple of heavy books, for at least 15 minutes or until the glue sets.

2. Repeat the above steps to make the other three panels.

making hinges for a screen

This incredible little hinge flexes in both directions. Follow these instructions if you plan to make a screen. If you wish to make a lantern, skip to Variation: Making a Lantern at the end of these directions.

materials
- Ruler
- White glue
- Glue brush
- 12 pieces of a strong, thin Japanese paper, cut to 1 x 2½ inches (use paper that is plain or matches the paper used in the panels, since the hinges will be visible)

1. Place two panels on your work surface, with the skewer side facing up. With the ruler, gently draw marks on the two vertical edges that will be joined together at 2½, 5, and 7½ inches.

2. Starting at the right edge at the top of the left panel, carefully brush glue on the top surface from 0 to 2½ inches and attach the left-hand edge of one of the paper strips. Apply glue from 5 to 7½ inches and attach another strip of paper.

3. Starting at the top of the left edge on the right panel, brush glue on the top surface from 2½ to 5 inches and attach the right-hand edge of one of the paper strips. Apply glue from 7½ to 10 inches and attach another strip of paper.

4. Crease all of the glued strips along the edge of the panels (figure 6).

5. Interlock the alternating strips on the two panels and flip both panels over, laying them on the work surface with the ¼-inch loose ends sticking up (figure 7). *Note:* Take care not to get glue on the middle section of the paper strips during the next step. If you do, the hinge will not move freely.

6. Crease the loose ends by folding them against the wood frames. Peek underneath the frames to determine which side the bottom of each strip is glued to and fold it over so that it is lying on top of the opposite panel. For example, if the bottom of the strip is glued to the left panel, the unglued part of the strip should be lying on top of the right panel, and the paper strip should look like an *S*. The next strip should lie over the opposite panel and look like a *Z*. Proceed down the panel, creasing the alternating paper strips.

7. Carefully apply glue to the back of each paper strip, working on one hinge at a time. Work down the panel and attach all of the hinges.

8. Lift the two panels and test the hinge—it should bend backward and forward.

9. Repeat steps 1 through 8 to join the two remaining panels to the screen. Place a straight edge along the bottom when you are joining panels to make sure they line up.

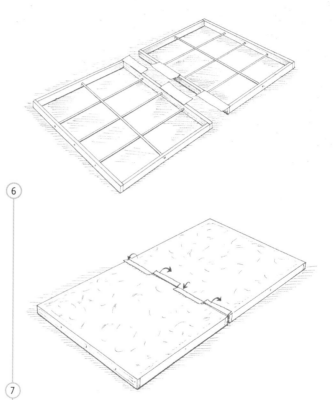

variation: making a lantern

To make a lantern, follow the instructions for Making Hinges for a Lantern (see Shadow Lantern project, page 33). (The hinges for a screen flex in both directions and are more complicated than the simple one-way hinges for a lantern.)

paper and incandescent light

There are so many wonderful ways to integrate paper with incandescent lighting. It can be as simple as draping a sheet of paper underneath a bare bulb or as complex as designing a paper shade to match a lighting fixture. In addition, many types of lights are suitable to use with paper, such as rope lights, battery-operated lanterns, and a wide variety of fluorescent and incandescent bulbs.

Paper is often a perfect and simple solution for softening the glare of a bulb. In this chapter you'll learn how to make lamps that are freestanding, as well as mounted on the wall and hung from the ceiling. *Note:* Before you start a project that involves electricity, read the information on safety, testing lampshades, lightbulbs, and wiring lamps in Lamp Basics.

luminaria

I spent many childhood Christmases in northern New Mexico, where luminaria lined the rooftops and walkways. Driving around to see the holiday lights in Santa Fe had an added sense of festivity. These luminaria are suitable decorations both indoors and out. Use them to line a walkway, provide the focal point for a centerpiece, or add ambience to mantel decorations.

This project is incredibly simple, so you can create one or more lanterns in a hurry before a party. If you have more time, try some of the techniques described in the Enhancing Paper chapter to create your own unique paper. If you make a series of lanterns, consider varying the heights of the luminaria for a more dramatic effect. Another plus: The battery-operated utility lights used in this project are a safe alternative to candles.

selecting the paper

Use paper that is sturdy, translucent, and decorative—this is the perfect project to show it off! If you want to use a fragile paper that will not stand on its own, line the paper with styrene to add structural support.

materials

- ¼-inch double-sided tape or white glue
- 13- x 8-inch paper (grain must run in the 8-inch direction)
- 4-inch diameter battery-operated utility light

1. Apply a strip of double-sided tape to the wrong side of one of the paper's short edges.

2. Remove the protective strip on the tape and place the bottom edge of the paper (the untaped side) on the edge of a utility light, making sure that the tape on the opposite edge is facing in toward the light (figure 1).

3. Wrap the paper around the light until it fits snugly. Carefully attach the tape to the other edge of the paper.

4. Repeat steps 1 to 3 to make more luminaria.

5. Arrange the lights, turn them on, and slip the shades over the lights. Remember to turn the lights off after you are done using them.

6. *Optional:* You could place two or three small pieces of tape on the rim of the light to secure the luminaria in place. However, you'll have to reach all the way inside the shade to turn the light on.

1

watermarked luminaria

I have a small product line of luminaria that I create from handmade cotton paper with watermarked designs. To make the designs, I cut the watermark images out of thin, adhesive-backed rubber and adhere them to the papermaking mold. When a sheet of paper is formed, it is thinner where the raised design is and thicker every-where else—this is what makes a watermark visible. I've also designed a wooden base that holds the paper's square shape and has a recessed hole for a glass tea light holder. My designs range from snowflakes to Celtic knots, which are lovely when illuminated by a candle. *Photos by James Dee.*

spinning lantern

This spinning lantern is a traditional Asian lighting device that has provided an almost magical pleasure for centuries. A pinwheel-topped cylinder of paper with decorative cutout shapes sits inside the lantern. When the lamp is turned on, the heat makes the cylinder spin, sending shadow pictures racing around the box-shaped lantern walls. A fully transparent lightbulb makes the light source seem smaller. Consequently, the shadows are stronger and more crisply defined.

A few specialty parts are required for this project and are available from The Lamp Shop (see Supply Sources). You can purchase an entire kit to make the store's version of a spinning lamp, which is slightly different from mine, or you can just purchase the hardware. You'll also need a little bit of patience and some wiring skills, but I'll guide you through it step by step. This project has several parts to it, but the results are worth the effort.

selecting the paper

Choose a sturdy, heavy-weight paper for the spinning mechanism on the lamp. The paper for the screen should be light in color and semi-translucent so that the shadows will be visible.

materials

- Pattern for pinwheel and cutouts (see page 129)
- Photocopy machine
- 2 pieces shade paper
- Craft knife
- Cutting mat
- Pushpin or needle
- ¼-inch double-sided tape
- Specialty lamp clip and snap
- Screen paper
- Standard A-type fully transparent lightbulb

making the pinwheel

1. Enlarge the pinwheel pattern (figure 1) and cut it out (see page 129 for a larger pattern). Trace the pattern onto the wrong side of one piece of the shade paper. This will eliminate the need to erase any marks, since they will be hidden from view. Be sure to transfer the small 'V's on each section onto the shade paper—these are the guides for folding the pinwheel.

2. Using a craft knife and a cutting mat, cut along all of the solid lines.

3. Mark the center point with a pushpin or needle to create a hole for the snap.

4. Apply the double-sided tape to the wrong side of each pinwheel section, from the 'V' mark to the point.

5. Working with the right side of the paper facing you, remove the double-sided tape protector on the point of one pinwheel section and fold it over so that the point is aligned with the 'V' mark on the section to the left (figure 2).

6. Repeat step 5 on all of the pinwheel sections.

7. Insert the snap into the center hole.

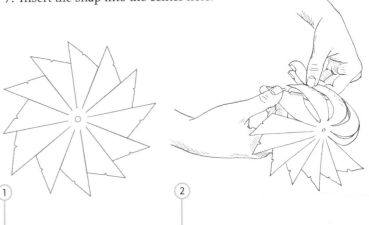

1   2

making the cutouts and attaching the pinwheel

1. To make the cutouts, you can use the pattern (figure 3) or come up with your own design (see page 129 for a larger pattern). Draw something freehand or consult a book of clip art to find interesting artwork.

2. Cut the second sheet of shade paper to 15 x 4½ inches. Cut out the shapes using a craft knife (figure 4).

3. Apply a piece of double-sided tape along the top, long edge of the wrong side of the cutout paper. Apply tape along one of the short sides of the cutout paper, also on the wrong side. This will be the seam.

4. Remove the adhesive protector from the longer strip of tape and lay the shade paper tape-side up on your work surface. Set one edge of the pinwheel on the adhesive so that it covers the entire ¼ inch of tape. Carefully roll the pinwheel top along the tape's edge, using it as a guide to attach the pinwheel and creating a cylinder as you roll it (figure 5).

5. When you get to the final edge, remove the adhesive protector from the short side and attach it to the other short side of the paper, making sure that it is straight and that the bottom edges of the paper are lined up.

making the screen

This is a simple superglue construction. If you are handy with wood and hand tools, you may want to finesse this design by creating real joints.

materials

- 4 pieces of ¼- x ¼-inch basswood, cut to 8-inch lengths
- 8 pieces of ¼- x ¼-inch basswood, cut to 6-inch lengths
- Handsaw
- Sandpaper
- Superglue for basswood
- Straight edge
- Triangle
- 4 pieces of screen paper, cut to 6½ x 6 inches
- White glue
- Small glue brush
- 1 piece of ¼- x 1-inch basswood, cut to 6½ inches with the ends mitered
- Porcelain socket with screws
- Screwdriver
- Drill

1. Cut the basswood lengths with a handsaw and sand any rough edges.

2. Lay two of the 8-inch lengths of basswood perpendicular to you on the table top. Set two of the 6-inch lengths between them, one at the top edges and one aligned so that the bottom edge of the basswood is 6 inches from the top of the uppermost 6-inch length.

3. Use superglue to adhere the pieces in place; use a straight edge and a triangle to make sure that the joints are square (figure 6).

4. Repeat steps 2 and 3 to make the second panel.

5. Set one panel on its side against the edge of a straight edge and set two of the loose 6-inch lengths of basswood perpendicular to the panel, lining them up with the 6-inch lengths that are already glued to that panel. Glue them in place, making sure that the angles are 90 degrees (figure 7).

6. Join the second panel to the two loose edges of the basswood, keeping everything square as you work.

7. Glue the last two 6-inch lengths to create the finished box.

attaching the paper

1. Attach a paper panel to each square frame on the sides of the box using white glue and a small glue brush. To do this, apply glue to the outside edges of one frame of basswood and carefully lay the paper on top of the glued area. Gently press along the glued edges, smoothing out any wrinkles or bubbles (figure 8).

2. Repeat step 1 on the remaining three panels.

assembling the lamp

You are nearing the finish line! *Ready:* Attach the socket to a crossbeam. *Set:* Wire the lamp. *Go:* Plug in the lamp and watch it spin.

1. Carefully make a 45- to 75-degree angle at the corners of the ¼- x 1-inch piece of basswood with a small handsaw or sandpaper. This creates a clean edge that won't be visible when the wood is installed inside the box.

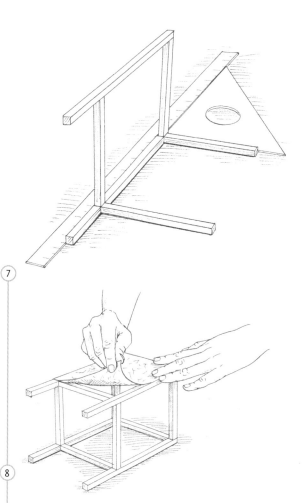

2. Wire the socket, following the steps on pages 123–126.

3. Center the socket on the shorter side of the strip of basswood (the side with the angles cut out) and mark the holes for the screws. Predrill the holes, if necessary, and attach the socket to the piece of basswood with a screwdriver (figure 9).

4. Turn the box upside down and pick an arbitrary side on the bottom of the frame. Measure it to find the center and make a mark horizontally, ½ inch from the center in both directions (figure 10). Make the same marks on the opposite panel. This creates a 1-inch guide for gluing the wood that holds the socket.

5. Apply a thin bead of superglue to the bottom edges of the wood with the socket, carefully slip it into the box, and then attach it to the frame.

6. Attach the specialty lamp clip to the bulb and screw the bulb into the socket. Carefully set the pinwheel assemblage on the needle on top of the lamp clip. (figure 11)

7. Turn on the lamp and watch it begin to spin as it warms up.

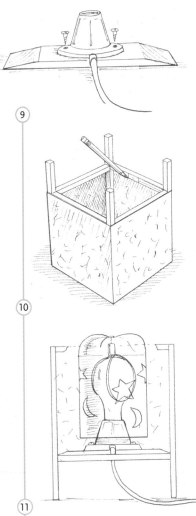

RESOLUTE

Douglas Varey was eager to start a lamp company after finishing his BFA in Industrial Design.

Around the same time, his friend, Brent Markee, created a lamp for an office holiday party that met with rave reviews. The two combined their talents and started working on Markee's product in the late 1980s.

Markee's lampshade had originally been made with an Italian watercolor paper. Varey and Markee wanted to design a shade that would have the beautiful glow of paper but be less fragile, so they began an epic materials search. Markee soon discovered Aramid, a product invented and manufactured by DuPont. Aramid is a synthetic carbon fiber that won't burn, is super tough, and looks like parchment paper. DuPont told them their lampshade idea was crazy—

they would never figure out how to make Aramid work as a shade, and besides, who would want a "paper light" anyway?

The duo proved DuPont wrong. Their company, RESOLUTE, which is based in Seattle, Washington, produces minimalist elegant shades. Their business continues to grow with new designs for paper lights and a glassblowing facility to make handblown lights. *Photos by Dan Langley.*

LEFT AND ABOVE: *RESOLUTE lamp designer Andrew Elliott wanted to create the illusion of paper penetrating the hoops and coming out the other side. Oddly enough, in his final product, called* Fugue, *it is actually the stainless-steel hoops that penetrate the paper shade.*

chochin
lantern

Chochin, a traditional portable lantern, is made of thin bamboo cane wound into a spiral on a removable

frame with paper glued to the outside of the bamboo. The lantern is collapsible and can be folded flat, making it easily portable. These lanterns, one of Japan's first forms of suspended lighting, were hung on Japanese shop fronts and bore the symbol or name of the business. Traditionally, the Japanese did not install lights on walls or ceilings, but today chochin are commonly used as ceiling lamps.

I have always been interested in how things are made, but I could never imagine the structure used to create this lantern. Another papermaker showed me how to create the armature and shade, and I was amazed. It is an elaborate process, but once you've constructed the armature, you can reuse it. The collapsible lantern that this process produces is quite special indeed. This project first appeared in my book *The Papermaker's Companion.*

selecting the paper

I recommend using a strong, thin, translucent paper. The paper needs to be manipulated, so it should be soft and flexible, too.

materials

- Photocopier
- Card stock
- ⅛-inch foam core
- Cutting knife
- Straight pins
- Scotch tape
- Thin basketry reed
- White glue
- Glue brush
- 7 strips of Japanese tissue or other strong paper, cut to ½ x 2 inches
- 7 small clamps (optional)
- Large sheet of shade paper
- Methyl cellulose glue (optional)
- Water mister (optional)
- String

making the lampshade structure

1. Use a photocopier to enlarge the patterns (figures 1 and 2) for the lantern's spokes and ribs (see page 130 for larger patterns). Cut out the lamp rib and spoke patterns and trace them onto card stock to make templates, and then cut out the templates. Note that the spoke's grooves must be ⅛ inch to fit the ribs.

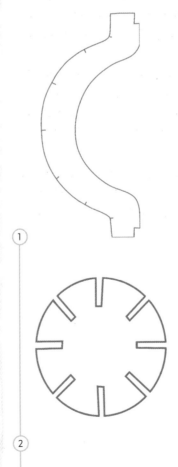

1

2

2. Trace two spokes and eight ribs onto a piece of foam core and cut them out using a sharp cutting knife. Trace the marks on the rib pattern onto the edges of each rib to indicate the reed spacing (figure 3).

3. Assemble the lamp form so that it resembles the diagram (figure 4). If anything is loose, stick straight pins into the foam core to hold things in place.

4. Carefully apply strips of Scotch tape to the edges of the ribs to prevent the paper from sticking to them during the gluing process.

5. Wrap a piece of reed around the top section of the lamp frame, at the place where it starts to curve. Cut a piece of reed so that it is as long as the lamp's circumference at this point plus ½ inch. Wrap the reed around the lamp frame again and mark where the ends overlap. Using a cutting knife, carefully slice the two ends of reed at a long, gradual incline. This gives them a flush joint (figure 5).

6. Carefully apply white glue with a glue brush to one side of a strip of Japanese tissue paper and wrap it around the reed joint. Place the reed ring on the lamp frame. You may want to fasten the ends of the reed together with a small clamp until the glue sets.

7. Repeat steps 5 and 6, measuring lengths of reed to fit around the ribs at each subsequent marking. Use straight pins to hold the rings of reed in place on the ribbed frame (figure 6).

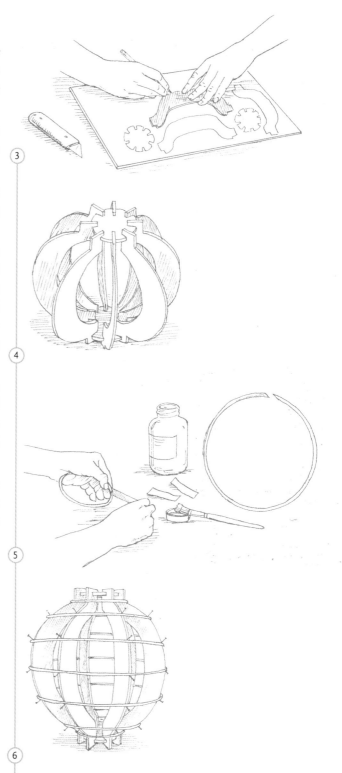

mounting a ceiling lamp

Ceiling fixtures are usually mounted directly to an electrical box in the ceiling. The shade can be attached to the lamp cord or can be suspended from its own threads or wires. Heavier fixtures, such as chandeliers, must be secured with a mounting strap; a threaded nipple secures the strap to the stem of the fixture. I find it easier to design paper shades that can be hung around or beneath ceiling fixtures to create an interesting effect, rather than trying to reinvent the fixture itself.

applying the paper

1. You can use a variety of papers to cover your lantern—most Japanese papers work well. Use the pattern (figure 7) to cut eight panels out of a thin, flexible sheet of paper (see page 130 for a larger pattern). Or try assorted papers cut or torn into various sizes and shapes to cover the form in a more random fashion. If you are using this technique, I recommend applying methyl cellulose glue where the paper overlaps.

2. Cover the lamp form with paper section by section. Remove the straight pins from one section and apply glue to the sections of reed. Place a piece of paper over the area, centering it over the two ribs (figure 8).

3. As you work, you will need to manipulate the paper a bit to compensate for the curvature of the form. You may even need to make tiny pleats or folds. Gently misting dry paper before applying it will make it a bit easier to manipulate, too.

4. Remove the straight pins from the segment directly across from the first section and apply glue to the reed. Apply a sheet of paper as in step 2.

5. Apply paper in sections to every other segment until you have covered four areas. Applying the paper in this fashion holds the rings in place.

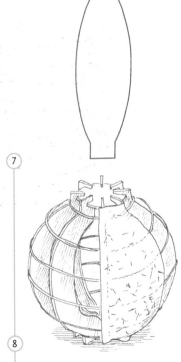

6. Cover the remaining sections with paper. In addition to applying glue to the reed strips, carefully apply a ¼-inch strip of glue along the two overlapping sides of the paper panels. Place a section of paper on the armature, overlapping the paper on both sides and tamping it down with your fingers or a brush to make sure it adheres to the adjacent sheet. Repeat this step until you have covered every section.

7. Allow the shade to dry overnight.

8. Remove the armature by pulling out the spokes, collapsing the ribs, and gently pulling the ribs out of the paper form.

9. If you plan to hang your lantern, tie a piece of string that is 10 inches long to the top reed ring in two places directly across from one another.

10. Apply glue to the extra ½ inch of all the sections left at the top and bottom of the lantern, wrapping and tucking the ends around the reed and gluing the paper to itself. Cut little slits when you work around the string.

hiding the cord

There are a number of decorative ways to hide an unsightly cord. Try covering the cord with ribbon woven with metal thread, which will allow you to wrap and tuck the ribbon in place. Or sew a narrow tube of fabric, insert the cord into it, and scrunch the fabric to produce a textured look. You can also make a paper tube out of the same paper you used for the lamp's shade.

night-light

Night-lights are the perfect solution for those of us who need a bit of illumination when we wake up in

the middle of the night. These decorative mini-sconces fit around standard electrical outlets and attach to a night-light fixture. They can be illuminated during the day too, adding a decorative touch of light to any room.

The Lamp Shop (see Supply Sources) carries a line of wire frames for night-lights that fit onto a clip. The kit comes with everything you need, including the night-light fixture and bulb. You can easily make your own patterns and wrap paper around these wire frames, using the techniques described for covering panel shades (see pages 99–101).

selecting the paper

Almost any paper will work for this project. Keep in mind that light will glow through a translucent paper but will be directed to the top and bottom openings of an opaque paper. The paper needs to wrap around the wire frame, so it can't be too stiff. If there is a design on your paper, lay out your pattern so that the design is oriented in the direction you desire.

materials

- Wire night-light frame (see figure 1, right, for example); night-light fixture with clip; and seven-watt night light bulb (available as a kit from The Lamp Shop)
- Card stock
- Ruler
- Tracing paper or photocopy machine
- Craft knife
- Shade paper

making the pattern

These instructions are for covering a two-panel night-light. If you are covering a night-light with three or more panels, follow the instructions for making panel lampshade patterns found on pages 98–99.

1. When covering the night-light shade panel by panel, I use two different (but similar) patterns. I start with a pattern for one panel (I arbitrarily picked the left panel), which will have seams on all four sides that wrap around the wire frame. The second pattern is for the right-hand panel and is slightly smaller, since the paper does not need to wrap around the central wire, which is already covered with paper (figure 2, right).

2. Set the left-hand panel face down on a piece of card stock. Lightly trace the panel just outside of the wires, keeping the pencil right at the edge of the wire. Use a ruler to draw over the lines to straighten them. Trace or photocopy this pattern so that you have two copies.

3. To create the left-hand panel pattern that wraps around all four wires, add a ⅛-inch seam to all four sides.

4. To create the right-hand panel pattern, add a ⅛-inch seam to the top, bottom, and right edges and a ⅛-inch seam to the left edge (this will cover the central wire).

5. Cut out the two patterns with a craft knife and label them "left panel" and "right panel." Test the patterns by placing them on the panels and making sure that each one has enough of a seam allowance to wrap around the wires.

6. Use the patterns and a pencil to trace each pattern onto the wrong side of the shade paper. Take care to orient each panel in the same direction on your paper if it has a directional design on it. Work on the front side of the paper, if necessary, and erase the pencil marks after cutting.

attaching the shade to the frame

1. Place the left panel of shade paper face down on your work surface. Apply glue to the front of the corresponding wire panel on the frame.

2. Carefully place the glued side of the wire frame onto the paper panel, centering it as you set it down (figure 3). Adjust it slightly, if necessary.

3. Turn the frame over and smooth out any wrinkles in the paper. Cut the corners of the shade at an angle, leaving about ⅛ inch from the wire intact.

4. Turn the panel over and lay it down again. Working on one wire at a time, use a micro spatula or plastic knife to gently lift the flaps and wrap them around the wires. Work quickly, so that the glue doesn't dry. If there is excess paper, gently prod it underneath the wire or push the excess up against the edge of the wire. (Overhanging paper will show when your shade is illuminated, so trim excess paper prior to gluing.)

5. Place a piece of scrap paper with a straight edge on top of the covered left-hand panel, ⅛ inch in from the covered central wire. Apply glue to the exposed strip and remove the scrap paper. Apply glue to the remaining uncovered wires.

6. Place the right-hand paper panel face down on your work surface. Set the glued side of the frame onto the shade paper, allowing ⅛ inch of overhang near the covered central wire.

7. Turn the frame over and check the fit, making sure that all the wires are covered. Press the ⅛-inch overhang firmly, so that the overlap sticks to the left-hand panel. Make adjustments and smooth out any wrinkles. Cut the corners of the shade at an angle, leaving about ⅛ inch from the wire intact.

8. Turn the panel over and lay it down again. Working on one wire at a time, use a micro spatula to gently lift the flaps and wrap them around the wires.

installing the night-light

1. Plug in the night-light fixture and attach the clip.

2. Set the night-light shade on the clip and flip the switch.

materials
- White glue
- Micro spatula or plastic knife
- Bone folder
- Straight edge

Alternative Designs

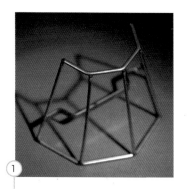

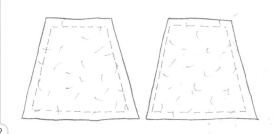

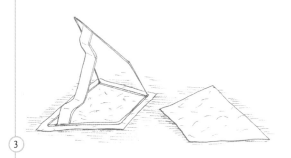

wall
sconce

You can create a unique wall sconce for any wall in your home without having to install a special fixture.

You will need to find a rope light, which is a fun, inexpensive string of lights encased in a flexible plastic tube that can be plugged into an outlet. Rope light is available from specialty lighting stores and is sold in multiples of 18-inch lengths (18 inches, 36 inches, 54 inches, and so on). It doesn't get hot, so it is safe to use with paper. It is also safe to use outdoors. The possibilities with rope light seem endless—try decorating with a long rope and twist or tie it into knots. This is a quick project once you've gathered the materials.

selecting the paper

Use a translucent or semi-translucent paper for this project. If the paper is very thin and fragile, then it is best to back it with styrene. The styrene will provide support and give it some structure.

materials

- 18-inch length of rope light with cord and plug
- Double-sided tape or wall tack
- 12 x 18-inch sheet of paper (backed with styrene, if necessary)
- 3 zip ties with loops (available from specialty hardware stores or electrical suppliers)
- 3 wood screws (and wall anchors, if necessary)
- Screwdriver
- Level

attaching the paper to the wall

1. Determine the position for the wall sconce on your wall, making sure that it hangs above an outlet and that the cord will reach the plug. Make small pencil marks to indicate where the rope light will hang.

2. Apply pieces of double-sided tape or wall tack along the 18-inch edges of the shade paper.

3. Attach one edge of the paper to the wall, to the left of where the rope light will hang.

installing the rope light

1. Attach the zip ties to the rope light at the top, center, and bottom, orienting them so that they will be flush with the wall when the rope light is mounted (figure 1).

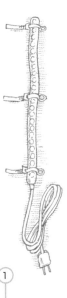

1

2. Mount the rope light to the wall by inserting screws into the loops of the ties (figure 2). Use the level to mount it so that the top and bottom edges of the rope light are flush with the edges of the paper.

3. Attach the other edge of the paper to the wall, to the right of the installed rope light.

4. To hide an unsightly electrical cord, see page 86, Hiding the Cord, for design ideas.

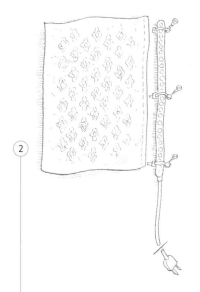

Therese Zemlin's *The Impossibility of the Previous Existence of Paradise and the Eternal Search for Equilibrium* was created with paper-covered armatures using the same method as chochin lanterns. The artist, who lives in Dorchester, Massachusetts, used her thoughts about the Garden of Eden, heaven and hell, and nudity as inspiration for this piece. There is also a reference to the Pagan Maypole and the notion of each person having a "double," a second self, or an evil twin. *Photos by Hunter Clarkson.*

panel lampshade

The structure of most lampshades is a wire frame covered with some sort of material, usually fabric or paper. Lampshade frames are available in a variety of shapes and sizes. One of the most common types is the panel shade, which has several rectangular or trapezoidal panels and provides an excellent structure for paper lampshades.

Most of the following lampshade projects require that you make a pattern first. Creating a pattern for a lampshade allows you to test the paper's fit before cutting the actual paper for the shade. It also helps to ensure that all of the panels are identical. Patterns are particularly helpful for producing multiple shades of the same size. Panel shade patterns are fairly simple to create because you can trace the wire frame. This technique involves covering the shade panel by panel, which gives you the option of alternating papers.

NOTE: Always test the heat safety of your lampshades before using them. See page 117 for more information.

selecting the paper

Any paper will work for this project. Keep in mind that light will glow through a translucent paper but will be directed through the top and bottom openings of an opaque paper.

materials

- Wire lampshade frame
- Large sheet of stiff paper
- Straight edge
- Tracing paper or photocopy machine
- Ruler
- Craft knife
- Cutting mat
- Binder clips
- Shade paper

making the pattern

When covering a shade panel by panel, you can use two different but similar patterns. Start with the pattern for the large panels, which will have a seam on all four sides that wraps around the wire. The second pattern is for the small panels, which do not need to wrap around the wire on the two sides that are already wrapped with paper. Use this panel-by-panel pattern for panel shades of any shape or size. Just make sure to cut out the correct number of pieces. The following directions are for a six-panel shade.

1. Set one panel of the wire lampshade frame on a piece of stiff paper and lightly trace the panel just outside of the wires, keeping the pencil right at the edge of the wire (figure 1). After tracing, use a straight edge to draw over the lines to straighten them. Trace or photocopy this sketch so that you have two copies of the basic panel shape.

2. To create the large panel pattern that wraps around all four sides of the wire panel, add a ⅜-inch seam to all four sides of one of the patterns.

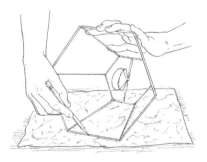

1

3. To create the small panel pattern, which wraps around the top and bottom wires but not the two sides (which will already be covered with paper), use the other copy of the panel pattern. Add a ⅛-inch seam to the top and bottom edges and an ⅛-inch seam to the two side edges.

4. Cut out the two patterns with a craft knife and a cutting mat and mark one "large panel" and the other "small panel." Place them on a panel of the wire frame with binder clips and make sure that each one has enough of a seam allowance to wrap around the wires.

5. Use the patterns and a pencil to trace three copies of each pattern onto the wrong side of the shade paper. Take care to orient each panel in the same direction on the paper if it has a directional design on it. To do this, you may need to work on the front side of the paper and erase the pencil marks after cutting out the pattern. Keep track of which panels are large and which are small.

covering the shade

These instructions are for covering a six-panel shade, but they will work for any shade with an even number of panels. If you used my technique of creating two panel sizes, start with the large panels.

materials

- Wire lampshade frame
- White glue
- Glue brush
- Panels cut out of shade paper
- Scissors
- Micro spatula, plastic knife, or wooden coffee stirrer
- Newsprint or scrap paper

testing your patterns

Always test your pattern by attaching it to the wire frame or rings with clips (binder clips work really well for both testing and covering the actual shade). After you clip the pattern onto the wire frame, examine all the areas that will wrap around and extend over each other, making sure that there is enough paper for overlap. Check the seams to see whether they will be even. Make any adjustments to your pattern before tracing it onto the actual paper you'll use for the shade.

1. Place the lampshade frame on your work surface. Apply glue with a glue brush to the front side of one of the panel frames (figure 2).

2. Place one of the large paper shade panels right-side down on your work surface. Carefully place the glued side of the wire frame onto the paper shade panel, centering it as you set it down. Adjust it slightly, if necessary.

3. Pick up the wire frame with the paper attached (it should be held in place by the glue) and turn it over. Smooth out any wrinkles where the panel is glued to the wire frame. Cut the corners of the panel at an angle, leaving ⅛ inch from the wire intact (figure 3).

4. Turn the panel back over and lay it down. Apply glue to the bottom overhanging flap of paper (see Gluing Tip on page 31), making sure that you cover the entire strip of paper with glue.

5. Using a micro spatula, a plastic knife, or a wooden coffee stirrer, gently lift the flap with glue on it and wrap it around the wire (figure 4). It should just cover the wire—if there is some excess and your paper is pliable, you should be able to gently prod it underneath the wire or push it up against the edge of the wire. Overhanging paper will show when the lamp is turned on, so trim any excess paper prior to gluing. Repeat this step to glue the three remaining flaps in place.

6. Repeat steps 1 to 5 to apply the large panels to every other panel on the frame.

7. After attaching all of the large panels, glue the small panels to the remaining uncovered panels. The sides of these panels glue directly to the panels that are already covered so be very careful when gluing (figure 5, opposite page).

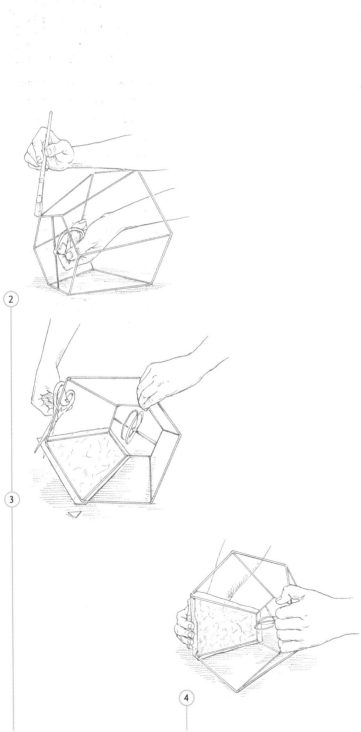

2

3

4

8. Place one of the small panels right-side down on a piece of newsprint or scrap paper on your work surface. Take two strips of scrap paper with straight edges and lay them on top of the panel, approximately ⅛ inch in from each of the side edges. Apply glue to the exposed ⅛-inch strips on the shade paper and remove the scrap paper. This will give you a narrow, neatly applied line of glue that will attach to the side edges of the frame. Work quickly, so that the glue doesn't dry.

9. Apply glue to the top and bottom wires of one of the frame panels (do not apply glue to the side wires, which are covered with paper). Carefully place the glued side of the wire frame onto the paper panel, centering it as you set it down. Adjust it slightly, if necessary.

10. Pick up the wire frame (the paper panel should be held in place by the glue) and turn it over. Smooth out any wrinkles where the panel is glued to the wire frame. Cut the corners of the panel at an angle, leaving an ⅛ inch from the wire intact.

11. Turn the panel back over and lay it down. Apply glue to the top edge of the paper panel, making sure that you have applied glue on the entire strip.

12. Using a micro spatula or another tool, gently lift the flap with glue on it and wrap it around the wire.

13. Repeat steps 11 and 12 on the bottom wire.

14. Repeat steps 8 to 13 to attach the rest of the small panels.

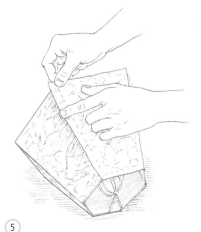

working around the bulb clip

On most wire frames, some sort of fitter wire connects to the top wire. When covering these sections with paper, attach the paper to the frame and, as you cut the angles on the paper's corners, cut a slit on both sides of the connecting wire as well. When you glue the paper to the wire frame, glue the little tab you created to the top wire (see below).

wraparound shade

This arc-shaped shade is glued to a rigid backing material to form a cone, and then attached to top and

bottom rings. Sometimes the rings are joined by struts, or side wires, which are soldered to hold the top and bottom rings together. In general, the top ring attaches the shade to the lamp base or the bulb in some fashion, and the bottom ring maintains the shape of the shade. Making wraparound shades from two loose rings can be tricky. A stiff backing material is needed to support a shade that doesn't have struts.

NOTE: Always test the heat safety of your lampshade before using it. See page 117 for more information.

selecting the paper

Any paper will work for this project. Keep in mind that light will glow through a translucent paper but will be directed through the top and bottom openings of an opaque paper. Thin paper is fine to use for this project, since it will be backed with styrene.

materials

- Straight edge
- Large sheet of stiff paper
- Protractor or triangle with right angle
- Top and bottom rings
- Ruler
- Extended compass
- Scissors or craft knife
- Pencil

making the pattern

I have come across a couple of different formulas for making patterns for wraparound lamps. This one uses geometry, and I find it the easier of the two for my brain. This method can be used for any shade height and any ring sizes, providing the top ring is smaller than the bottom ring. Follow the instructions below, using the diagram (figure 1) as a guide. If the pattern is created with accuracy, a beautiful shade will result.

1. Use a straight edge to draw line AB across a sheet of paper near the bottom edge.

2. Mark point C near the center of the line. Starting at point C, use a triangle to draw a right angle to AB, running all the way to the top of the paper. This is line CD.

3. Locate the center of the top and bottom rings and use a ruler to measure the diameter of each ring from the outside. These measurements should be precise. Divide the diameter in half to obtain the radius of each ring.

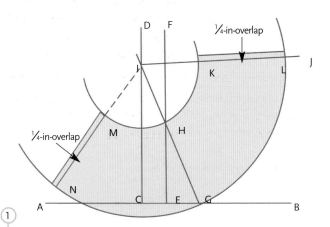

1

4. Starting at point C on line AB, mark point E at a distance equal to the radius of the top ring. Line CE equals the radius of the top ring. From point E, draw a line at a right angle to line AB to create line EF. Line EF is parallel to line CD.

5. Starting at point C on line AB, mark point G at a distance equal to the radius of the bottom ring. Line CG equals the radius of the bottom ring.

6. Decide on the side length of the shade. (The side length is the length of the side of the shade from the bottom outside edge of the bottom ring to the top outside edge of the top ring. This measurement is different than the height of the shade, which is the vertical distance from the top to the bottom of the shade. See figure 2.) Place one end of the ruler at point G and the other end on line EF at the side length you have determined. Mark that point H. Draw a line that connects points G and H and continues to cross line CD. Mark this point where the line crosses CD point I.

7. From point I, draw a line out to the right side of the paper, creating line IJ. The angle between line IJ and line CD is not important.

8. Using an extended compass with the point set on I, draw an arc with radius IH, cutting line IJ, and label the intersectioon of the arc and line IJ point K. Set the compass point on I again and draw an arc with radius IG, cutting line IJ, and label the point where the arc intersects line IJ point L.

9. Mark the top ring with a pencil at one point. Place the ring on edge so that the pencil mark is on point K and carefully roll the ring around the small arc until the pencil mark has made a complete rotation. Mark this place on the arc point M.

10. Mark the bottom ring with a pencil at one point. Place the ring so that the pencil mark is on point L and carefully roll the ring around the large arc until the pencil mark has made a complete rotation. Mark this place on the arc point N.

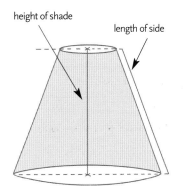

height of shade

length of side

2

lampshade terminology

It is important to use the proper vocabulary when speaking lampshade. The arc pattern is the template from which the arc is drawn onto the lampshade paper. The arc is the main body of a wraparound lampshade after it has been cut out and before it is attached to the wire rings. The shade is what it is called after the arc has been glued to the rings.

materials

- Top fitter wire ring
- Bottom wire ring
- Steel wool or sandpaper
- Rust-proof spray paint
- Scissors
- Adhesive-backed styrene
- Arc pattern
- Shade paper
- Bulldog clips
- Ruler
- Divider
- Art eraser
- Wax paper
- Scrap paper
- Glue brush
- Quik or PVA white glue
- Weights (a jar filled with grains works well)
- $\frac{5}{8}$-inch cotton or rayon-blend ribbon, $\frac{13}{16}$-inch cotton twill, $\frac{1}{4}$-inch water-activated paper tape, or similar width cotton twill tape, yarn, thread, or cord (optional)
- Compass
- Sharp scissors

11. Draw a line connecting points N and M, extending it to cut through line CD (see the dashed line on figure 1). If your work is accurate, the line will also go through point I. If the work is not accurate, the cone will be lopsided—go back and carefully check all your measurements.

12. The portion of the diagram between the two arcs, KLNM (see the shaded portion on figure 1), is the pattern for the wraparound shade. Add ¼ inch at each end for overlap. Cut out the pattern with a scissors or craft knife and check the fit with the rings (see Testing Your Patterns on page 99).

13. It is particularly important with wraparound shades to test the pattern before cutting the actual shade paper. If you've made a mistake, it is easier to adjust the pattern rather than cut a new shade.

14. The fit of an arc to the wires is unique. For the most accuracy, use a pattern only once after you've clipped and marked the seam overlap.

preparing the wire frames

I spray my wire frames with a clear acrylic spray or spray paint to keep them from rusting. If you choose to do this, work in a well-ventilated area and apply two or three coats. If you are working on more than one shade, coat several frames at once. Set them outside on newspaper and spray all of them on one side. When they are dry, turn them over and spray them on the other side.

covering the shade

Covering a wraparound shade correctly depends on how well you traced and cut the pattern. However, I'll show you a way to fix a minor error by adjusting the seam, if necessary.

preparing the rings

1. Look at all of the welded joints on the wire rings and clean off any burrs with steel wool or sandpaper. Place both rings on a level surface and make sure they lie flat. If a ring is not flat, let half of the ring extend over the edge of your worktable and gently bend the ring to straighten it.

2. Apply three coats of clear or colored rust-proof paint (it is easier to see that the frame is completely covered with paint if you use a color).

cutting the backing material and shade paper

1. Use scissors to cut out a rectangular piece of adhesive-backed styrene that is slightly larger than the arc pattern. Place the styrene on your work surface, with the adhesive side facing up. Trace the arc pattern onto the peel-off paper side of the styrene and carefully cut it out (figure 3).

2. Cut a rectangular piece of shade paper that is slightly larger than the piece of styrene.

3. Place the shade paper on the work surface with the wrong side facing up. Peel up one edge of the adhesive protector, removing only an inch or so. Adhere that edge to the shade paper, positioning it so that the styrene fits on the shade paper.

re-covering an old wraparound shade

If you are re-covering an existing wraparound shade, carefully remove the old covering, keep it intact, and use it as a pattern. Before taking it apart, though, check whether there is enough overlap at the seam and be sure to include any overlap in your pattern. Remove any trims so that you get down to the basic shape, and take care not to damage it. Place the old shade on the wrong side of your new lamp's paper and trace it (see below). If there isn't enough overlap, extend the pattern to make a $\frac{1}{2}$-inch seam. If the shade has struts, create a pattern using the method for panel shades (see pages 98–99).

wraparound cylindrical shades

It is much easier to make patterns for cylindrical (or drum) shades, since the top and bottom rings are the same size. First, determine the circumference of the rings (the length around the perimeter of the ring) and add ½ inch for the seam. Using a ruler, draw a line on the long side of the pattern paper near the top. Next, determine the height of the shade (it can be any height you want) and draw a line parallel to the first line at that distance (make the second line a bit longer). Use a square or a triangle to connect the two lines at right angles starting at the two end points on the first line to create a rectangular pattern. Then, follow the directions for covering a wraparound shade.

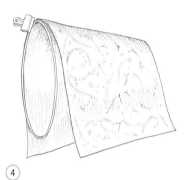

4

5

4. Carefully pull off the adhesive protector, removing it from the styrene and attaching it to the shade paper. Be sure to smooth out the paper as you work. Cut the shade paper to fit the styrene and complete the arc.

5. Transfer the markings from the pattern onto the back of the arc. Mark the center front of the paper at the top and bottom as well as the estimated back-seam overlap.

fitting the arc

1. Hold the bottom wire ring in one hand and let it hang down. With the other hand, hold the arc (styrene-backed shade paper) at the bottom center point, with the right side facing up. Place the bottom center point of the arc on the wire ring, right at the edge, and clip it in place with a bulldog clip. Place the clip at a 45-degree angle so that it touches both the arc and the wire ring (figure 4).

2. Move the arc and wire toward the left and attach another clip. Continue in this fashion until you reach the back seam. Return to the center and fit the right half of the arc into the wire ring. Overlap the back seam, left over right, and fasten it with a clip. Look over your work and make sure that there are no gaps and that the edge of the arc is flush with the wire ring. Set the arc upright on your work surface, with the center front facing you.

3. Hold the top wire ring by the fitter wire and place it just inside the top edge of the arc. Clip the ring at the center front.

4. Working to the right, clip the arc to the wire as you go, until you reach the back seam. Return to the center front and work around to the left. Overlap the back seam, right over left, and secure it with a clip (figure 5).

5. Check your work to make sure that you have a good fit. There should be no gaps between the arc and the rings and the arc should not protrude beyond the rings. Make adjustments, if necessary.

marking the seam

1. Stand the arc upright with the bottom edge down and the seam facing you. Put a light pencil mark on the outside of your shade at the top and bottom edges of where the seam overlaps. Remove the clips and set the rings aside (figure 6).

2. Place the arc on your work surface with the right side facing up and the pencil marks for the seam overlap on your right. Connect the two marks with a ruler and examine whether the overlap is straight.

adjusting a crooked seam

1. If the distance between the pencil marks and the edge of the back seam is noticeably different at the top and the bottom, use a divider to measure the shorter distance between the pencil mark and the back seam edge. For example, if the distance at the top edge is shorter, let's call that distance A.

2. Duplicate this measurement from the pencil mark at the bottom arc edge toward the seam and mark this point B.

3. Draw a straight line connecting points A and B to create a back seam overlap that is the same width from top to bottom.

4. Recheck the measurements and then cut along the line to remove the excess back seam allowance.

6

gluing the arc

1. Place the arc on your work surface with the wrong side facing up and the bottom of the arc closest to you. The back seam overlap will be on your right. Use an art eraser to remove any pencil markings on the back of the arc, except for the seam marks. Place a small piece of wax paper underneath the back seam overlap to protect the tabletop from glue. Place a piece of scrap paper with a straight edge along the marks for the back seam overlap. The paper should be on your left, exposing just the seam.

2. Using a brush, apply glue to the back seam overlap, starting on top of the scrap paper and brushing out onto the wax paper beneath, so that the entire seam is covered with glue. Remove the scrap paper and throw it away immediately, so that the glue doesn't get on anything else. Line up the top left-hand edge of the arc with the pencil mark on the right-hand side and secure it with a clip placed parallel to the edge of the arc. Make sure the overlap just covers the pencil mark, so that it is hidden. Line up the bottom left-hand edge of the arc with the pencil mark on the right-hand side and fasten it with a clip. Press down with your fingers along the seam edges.

3. Lay the arc seam-side down on wax paper and remove the clips. Press again with your fingers along the seam. Clean off any excess glue with a damp paper towel. Place small weights along the seam and let it dry for 15 to 20 minutes (figure 7).

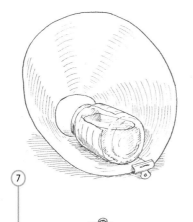

7

8

gluing the rings to the arc

1. Stand the arc on your work surface with the top of the arc resting on the table. Apply a thin line of glue around the inside bottom edge of the arc. Rotate the arc as you work.

2. Place a clip at the back seam, avoiding contact with the glue, and make sure it is parallel to the edge of the arc. Position the arc so that the back seam is facing away from you. Carefully set one side of the ring between the handles of the clip.

3. Ease the bottom wire ring into the inside edge of the arc at the center front. Fasten it with a clip at a 45-degree angle. Place three or four clips to the left and the right of the center clip (figure 8).

4. Lift and remove the ring from the clip at the back seam. Ease the ring into place and fasten it with more clips at 45-degree angles.

5. Turn the arc over, with the clips on the bottom of the arc resting on your work surface. Use a glue brush to apply glue to the top inside edge of the arc.

6. Lift the bottom of the arc and slip the top fitter wire ring onto the table underneath the arc. Reach down from the top of the arc, grasping the top ring by the fitter wire, and carefully draw it upward until it is even with the top edge of the arc. Fasten the center front with a clip at a 45-degree angle. Adjust the ring to fit evenly with the top edge of the arc. Continue fastening the ring to the arc with clips all around the top edge (figure 9).

9

binding the shade

There are many ways to attach the wires to the rings. Probably the most common is with a binding material, such as ⅝-inch grosgrain ribbon, ¹³⁄₁₆-inch cotton twill, or ¼-inch paper tape, but you can use cotton twill tape, yarn, thread, or cord, as well. The binding should roll over the wire ring and tuck into the groove where the ring and the arc meet inside. The gauge, or thickness, of the wire and the width of the binding material will determine the correct placement of a guideline to make the application of the binding accurate.

10

1. Rest the shade on your work surface with the top facing up.

2. Use a drafting compass to draw a line along the top edge of the shade, rotating the shade as you draw (figure 10).

3. Position the shade with one-third of the bottom hanging over the edge of your work surface. Draw a line with the drafting compass around the bottom edge of the shade, rotating the shade as you draw.

4. Cut a piece of binding material a couple of inches longer than the circumference of the top ring of the shade. Use sharp scissors to square off one end of the binding.

5. Apply glue to the lower half of the first 2 or 3 inches of the binding, starting at the cut end.

creating holes for lacing

If you want to lace the shade (see below) rather than attach a binding material, you'll need to pierce the lacing holes after you've backed the paper with styrene. The easiest way to make the lacing holes is to run both edges of the arc through an unthreaded sewing machine set on the widest straight stitch possible. This creates small holes for thread (I like waxed linen thread, which comes in a variety of colors). Use the edge of the arc as the guide for the sewing machine foot and stitch from end to end. If you need larger holes to stitch something wider, such as raffia, use a small hole punch instead.

6. Working from the back seam at the top of the shade, position the binding ¼ inch to the left of the seam overlap (figure 11). The bottom edge of the binding should just cover the line. Press it into place with your fingers, holding for a minute or so to let the glue set.

7. Hold the binding material away from the shade and apply glue to the lower half of the inner surface of the next 9 to 12 inches (figure 12). Attach the binding material to the shade, using the drawn line as a guide, and press it into place. Repeat this step, working with 9- to 12-inch sections, until you reach the back seam.

8. With the back seam as your guide, use sharp scissors to cut away the excess binding perpendicular to the edge of the shade, so that the binding will overlap and end at the shade overlap. Apply glue to the full width of the binding material at the back seam and press it into place. Let it dry for 10 minutes.

9. Use sharp-tipped scissors to make a small, narrow V in the binding material at all of the points where the fitter wires connect to the wire rings. Do not cut too close to the wire ring.

10. Apply a thin, even coat of glue to the wire ring and the inside of the entire top half of the binding material (figure 13).

11. Roll and mold the binding over the top wire with both hands, rotating the shade as you work. Smooth the binding material as you go along to create a clean finish. Hold the shade by the top fitter wire, reach inside from underneath the shade, and crease the edge with your fingernail. Press the binding material into the groove where the shade and the ring meet. Remove any excess glue with a wet paper towel.

12. Repeat steps 1 through 11 (omitting step 9) to bind the bottom edge of the lampshade to the wire ring.

NOTE: Always test the heat safety of your lampshades before using them. See page 117 for more information.

galbraith & paul

While in college studying painting, Liz Galbraith apprenticed with a papermaker and her fascination

with handmade paper turned into passion. After college, she spent time working and studying with various papermakers around the country. Inspired by Isamu Noguchi's lamps, she decided to design a line of lighting fixtures using her own handmade papers. To learn more, she headed to Japan on a study tour of the country's papermaking methods and decorative techniques.

Today, Galbraith creates lamp designs for her own patterned papers and her partner, Ephraim Paul, manages their business. Their company, based in Philadelphia, Pennsylvania, started out small in the 1980s, when lamps as an art form were scarce. They showed their lamps at American Craft Council craft fairs, and business took off. Within two to three years, their lamps were sold in shops all over the United States. They and their staff do everything, including forming the paper one sheet at a time using a Japanese stenciling technique, assembling the lamps, and attaching the shades to the frames.

Now, after more than 10 years, Galbraith & Paul lamps are sold in small craft stores, high-end furniture stores, and mail-order catalogs. Galbraith & Paul have also designed the lighting for such places as New York's swanky W Hotel and the National Arbor Foundation's conference center. *Photo by Steven Belkowitz.*

lamp basics

safety issues

Always make sure your lampshades are safe by:
1. Creating a design so the bulb isn't too close to the shade. Make the shade large enough so that it doesn't get too hot.
2. Selecting quality materials. Even though a shade may look nice at first, in time the material may yellow, become brittle, and fall apart.
3. Leaving an opening at both the top and the bottom of the shade, so that air can circulate and heat doesn't become trapped.

safety

You must think about safety when working with paper and electricity, since paper is flammable. However, if you follow these few precautions, you do not need to worry that your shades will catch fire. Much of the following information is for those interested in producing multiple lamps for sale. Although it is of utmost importance to create safe lighting fixtures, some of these items will not apply to crafters making just one lamp.

In the United States, Underwriters Laboratories Inc. inspects all electrical products that are marketed. Most commercial shades have little stickers on them that say UL tested or UL approved. All electrical appliances must be approved before they can be installed and sold. This is part of being "up to code." The information included here is merely an introduction to the safety issues surrounding the production of paper shades and is not meant to replace UL testing. For a full and proper understanding of these issues, contact Underwriters Laboratories in your state.

how hot is too hot?

The temperature limit for paper, wood, and ordinary fiber is 194°F (90°C) when the maximum room temperature is 86°F (30°C). This means that the surface temperature of the hottest spot on the inside of the shade cannot exceed 194°F (90°C). The shade temperature should not be confused with the air temperature immediately adjacent to the inside surface, since the shade may be absorbing and dissipating heat.

Usually, shades that have an open top never get close to 194°F, which is quite hot. Most people can't even place their hands on a surface that exceeds 92°F (32°C), and water boils at 212°F (100°C). However, for the temperature reading to remain accurate, you must ensure that the paper is securely mounted to the shade's frame. Otherwise, if someone bumps the lamp, the paper may come off the frame and rest against the bulb.

If the opening at the top of the shade is small, heat may collect there. Usually, the hottest spot is the point on the shade that is the shortest distance from the bulb. You can measure the surface temperature by taping thermocouples to the inside of the shade. Turn the lamp on and, once the temperature has stabilized, record the temperature with a digital thermometer. Although it won't be as accurate, you can also record the surface temperature with a glass thermometer or a digital thermometer.

the effect of heat on paper

Safety regulators are not concerned with the effect that heat may have on a material's appearance. For instance, your shade may pass all of the necessary heat tests but after a while may turn yellow, become brittle, and fall to the floor. In that case, the lamp is not a fire hazard but is poorly made. The paper's long-term durability is usually not a safety issue, unless the falling shade can become too hot or injure someone.

testing paper shades

To test your lampshade, follow these guidelines:

1. Use a higher wattage bulb for testing purposes. If the shade is designed for a 60-watt bulb, test the shade first with a 100-watt bulb. If the shade passes the temperature test, you have an extra safety factor. If it fails, try again using a 60-watt bulb.

2. Record the room temperature. If it is lower than 86°F, add the difference to the test result. For example, if the room temperature is 77°F, you must add 9°F to the temperature recorded on the hottest spot of the inside of the shade.

3. Although it is not required, leave an extra safety factor. The maximum allowable temperature is 194°F, but use a lower wattage bulb if the shade temperature exceeds 176°F.

4. Always leave an opening at both the top and the bottom of the shade so that heat is not trapped and air can circulate. As hot air rises and escapes from the top of the shade, cool air will be drawn in from the bottom of the shade.

going into production

If you plan to sell your lampshades, you need to obtain UL approval. Everything that leaves a production shop should be UL approved—most lighting stores will not purchase light fixtures that are not UL approved, and electricians can lose their licenses if they install light fixtures that are not approved.

On the other hand, I often see handmade paper lampshades with no approval labels in specialty stores. The cost to obtain UL approval is a couple thousand dollars plus a few hundred-dollar yearly fee (which pays for the unannounced spot checks), as well as the cost of special UL labels. And that is just for the shades. There are other standards regarding the wiring of light fixtures that I will not discuss here. The point is that these are matters of legal liability if your lamp causes a fire.

lanie kagan

Lanie Kagan, of New York City, never studied industrial design, but she has a successful business, called Luz Lampcraft, that

creates custom lamps for such stores as Victoria's Secret and Aveda. It all started 10 years ago, when Kagan was working as a graphic designer for a store in New York City that was about to go national. She started playing around with some lamp designs, and the store liked them so much that they asked her to produce them for sale. She felt the lamps were too labor intensive and that she couldn't make a profit making them, so she said no.

Three years later, as the graphic design industry became more and more computer oriented, Kagan realized she didn't want to sit at a computer all day. So, against her common sense, she started making potential home-décor products in her apartment. At first, Kagan's background in painting got her thinking about making painted canvas window

shades. These didn't make sense as a product though, since windows are not a standard size. So she went back to designing lamps.

Kagan visited a local paper store and was intrigued by the variety of paper that was available. The papers suggested shapes and lampshade designs to her. But she still needed something to serve as a frame. After finding an old wire lamp at a flea market, she did a little research and discovered the wire-forming industry. She found a wire former to produce the frames that she designed. Then she attached paper directly to the frames to create the lampshades.

Kagan attended her first trade show six months later and got a large order, which justified renting a studio space. Kagan spent the next six years growing her business, hiring employees, and selling

her lamps to stores around the country. But she still had cash flow problems. So she gave herself six months to a year—if business didn't get better, she would quit.

That's all it took. Within the year, not one but two companies asked her to design lamps for them. This worked out to her advantage. The two companies were fighting for her to join their ranks, and one offered to buy her 14 best-selling lamps, which they started manufacturing in Taiwan. Kagan was able to

stop selling wholesale and concentrate on a custom-design business.

Now she designs a group of lamps that she shows at the International Contemporary Furniture Fair in New York City each year. Architects and designers hire her to produce similar lamps in various shapes and sizes. Her primary shade material continues to be paper. Kagan's desire to follow her creative spirit and her willingness to take risks have paid off. *Photo by Michael Kozmiuk.*

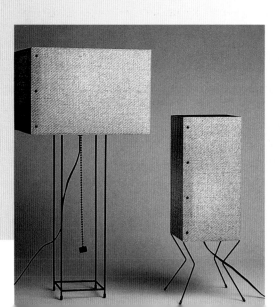

fireproofing materials

I know that there are people who use fireproof materials for their lampshades. These materials are not required by Underwriters Laboratories Inc. If your shade does not pass the temperature test, it's not safe, regardless of any fireproof material you may use. However, in the theater industry, materials must be fireproof. If your work is being displayed in a public space, you may be required to fireproof it. See the Supply Sources for useful resources.

types of lightbulbs

Lightbulbs can be clear, frosted, coated, or colored to provide different qualities of light. Bulbs are available in different wattages too. The higher the wattage, the more illumination a bulb will provide and the more electricity it will use.

Always look at your lamp before buying a replacement bulb. Consider what you need, then check the size of the socket and its recommended maximum wattage. This information is usually found on a sticker near the socket of light fixtures. Never use a bulb that exceeds the socket's maximum recommended wattage. If you do, the heat produced could char a paper shade, melt a plastic globe or shade, or damage the wire insulation. Because air space is essential, avoid using a bulb that is too large for the lamp or the shade fixture.

Lightbulbs come in a range of shapes and sizes. The most important thing to remember with paper shades is that you can't use a bulb that gets too hot, since paper is flammable (as are most shade materials). I recommend using 40 watts or less for paper shades. Be sure to test the heat safety of paper shades with lightbulbs (see page 117). Also, make sure that the bulb is at least 3 inches away from the shade in all directions.

be careful

You may be tempted to use a halogen or quartz lamp because of its small size or interesting shape. However, these lamps are very hot and have special requirements, so they should never be used with paper. The risk of causing a fire with these lamps is much greater than with incandescent lamps, even if they don't have paper shades. Some halogen bulbs are required to have a protective covering to catch shattered pieces should the bulb break. The covering also protects flammable materials and hands from touching a hot bulb.

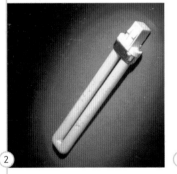

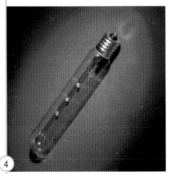

favorite bulbs for paper shades

a guide to bulbs

This list includes my favorite bulbs for use with paper shades, but this is by no means a complete inventory. I have intentionally omitted any type of bulb that is too hot to use near paper.

a-types

A-types, which fit medium-based sockets, are the most common lightbulbs used in standard lamps and light fixtures. A-type bulbs used with paper shades should not exceed 40 watts.

candelabra

Candelabra (figure 1) are used to provide accent lighting and fit medium-based and candelabra-type sockets. Candelabra bulbs used with paper shades should not exceed 40 watts.

fluorescent bulbs

Fluorescent bulbs (figure 2) shed up to six times more light per watt of power and last five times longer than incandescent bulbs do. They are an economical choice for areas where bright light is needed for long periods of time, such as kitchens and workshops.

g (globe)

Globe bulbs (figure 3) usually frame makeup mirrors and are used in hanging fixtures. They fit medium-based and candelabra-type sockets. Globe bulbs are actually more like fixtures in and of themselves, but paper shades can be placed below or around a hanging globe. Globe bulbs used with paper shades should not exceed 40 watts.

night-lights

These are small, low-wattage bulbs used in plug-in fixtures to illuminate hallways or rooms at night. They are also used in some Christmas lights. The bulbs fit medium-based and candelabra-type sockets and come in 4, 7, and 7½ watts.

t (tubular)

Tubular bulbs (figure 4) are usually used in medium-intensity desk lamps. They can also be mounted above picture frames and in the canopy of an aquarium. These bulbs fit medium-based sockets and range in brightness from 15 to 40 watts.

lamp bases

Making a lamp isn't just about the shade; most lamps need a base, too. In this section, you'll learn how to select a base to match your shade (or vice versa) and figure out how all of the parts fit together. If you are restoring an old lamp and the base is still intact, hang onto it. To update the base, try painting it, applying decoupage, or using another decorative technique.

Garage sales and antique stores are great places to find old lamp bases. Since home decorating is becoming more popular, some stores sell bases and shades separately. You can make your own base from wood, ceramics, or other materials, or you can hire a local craftsperson to do it.

shade-to-base proportion

When designing a lamp, the shade should be proportionate to the base. A general guideline is that the diameter of the base of the shade should be approximately equal to the height of the base. Color, scale, and style should also be considered, so that the base and shade are in harmony with each other. Of course, your own aesthetic is important, as well.

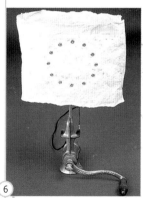

found objects

Many found objects can be converted into lamp bases. I once did a series of lamps with old tools and bells as bases (figures 5, 6, and 7, lamps by Helen Hiebert; photos by James Dee). I've also used terra-cotta pots. Household items, such as teapots and jars, can be converted into lamp bases, too. The parts for making these conversions are readily available from lamp suppliers.

anatomy
of a lamp

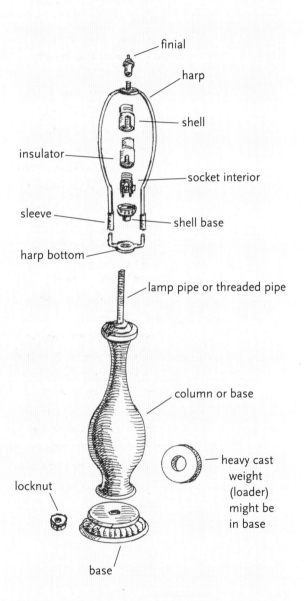

finial

harp

shell

insulator

socket interior

sleeve

shell base

harp bottom

lamp pipe or threaded pipe

column or base

heavy cast weight (loader) might be in base

locknut

base

A vase can be easily converted into a lamp base with just a few parts. Luckily, there is a special socket that prevents the need to drill a hole for the cord, which could damage the vase (figure 8). Vase caps are available in diameters ranging from 1¼ to 8½ inches. See pages 123–126 for specific instructions on wiring a lamp.

If the neck of your vase or other object doesn't fit an adapter, you can cut a plug from cork or wood to fit the neck. You can also purchase a base plate, which can be drilled and attached to the plug, and the socket can then be screwed onto the base plate. Parts for all of these adaptations are available from The Lamp Shop (see Supply Sources).

sockets

Most lamps are fitted with medium-base sockets designed for bulbs of up to 300 watts (I recommend no more than 40 watts for paper shades, though). Sockets with smaller bases, such as the intermediate base and the tiny candelabra socket, are designed to hold decorative, low-wattage bulbs. Low-wattage systems also have smaller sockets.

Sockets have two screw terminals or two pre-attached wires that are soldered or riveted on (figure 9). All sockets have a metal tube, which is often threaded, and a contact tab inside the socket. The outer casing is made of metal, plastic, or porcelain. For outdoor use, plastic, porcelain, and rubber offer durability, resistance to dampness, and maximum safety.

8

9

Sockets vary in the way they are mounted to the fixture. A lamp socket, for instance, has a cap that screws onto the center pipe of a lamp. You'll need a socket that fits the type of bulb you are using. You'll also need to decide how you plan to turn the lamp on and off. If you can't reach inside the shade to turn the lamp on, you can install a switch on the cord and use a keyless socket.

wiring and rewiring lamps

Wiring a lamp seems like a daunting and dangerous task to many of us. In fact, the process is very simple and, if you do it correctly, quite safe. If, after reading these directions, you are still mystified and wary of electrocuting yourself, an electrician or someone at a local lamp or hardware store can easily help you.

Whether you are refurbishing an old lamp that has been sitting in your garage or assembling a new creation, the instructions for wiring are the same. Basic wiring is the same for any lamp, though there are subtle differences. For example, the threading of the cord varies for table, floor, and ceiling fixtures. Two good sources of information are *Lighting and Electricity* and *Antiques on the Cheap,* from which the following is excerpted (see Recommended Reading).

wiring a table lamp

If a lamp doesn't work, the problem can be in one of only three places: the plug, the cord, or the socket. Unless the lamp is rather new, you may as well replace all three parts while you're at it. Before you start, however, study the illustration on page 122 to familiarize yourself with lamp terminology.

unplug it!

Here are a few safety precautions to take before wiring a lamp:

1. Never work on a lamp (or any electrical object) when it is plugged in.

2. Look at the plug. A plug with prongs of different sizes is a polarized plug. The wide prong of the plug is the neutral side. The wire leading from the wide prong is usually ribbed or marked with writing and connects to the silver screw in the socket. The unmarked wire is the hot wire, which attaches to the brass screw in the socket.

Never switch the wires on a plug. The lamp may work, but if you touch the socket, you'll be shocked. Literally. When a lamp is wired properly, the on/off switch interrupts the current-carrying hot wire, so that no power flows through it when the lamp is off.

test your wiring

In electrical work, it is important to make sure the wiring connections are safe by double checking your work. The wire ends that are looped around a terminal screw must be mechanically and electrically secure so that the current will flow smoothly from one part of the circuit to another. A continuity tester sends a small current through a circuit to determine whether its electrical path is intact.

To test for continuity, attach an alligator clip to one end of the circuit (the terminal screw on a switch or a plug prong, for example) and touch the probe to the other end (the other terminal screw on the switch or the bare cord wire). If the circuit is complete, the bulb will glow, indicating that your wiring is good (see below left). If the light doesn't glow, there is a break in the circuit. You can purchase continuity testers from electrical suppliers and specialty hardware stores.

materials

- Lamp
- Screwdriver
- 6–8 feet of flat lamp cord
- Craft knife or razor blade
- New socket (if necessary)
- Automatic plug to match color of lamp cord
- Replacement felt
- White glue
- Scissors

1. Unplug the lamp and remove the harp, since it's easier to take the shell off the socket if the harp is out of the way. Lift the two little sleeves where the top attaches to the bottom of the harp, and squeeze the harp near this attachment to remove the top part.

2. Take the old socket apart. Look at the socket where the shell meets the cap. You'll see the word *press* near the switch opening. Push on this with your thumb and tilt the shell toward the opposite side. The shell will come off, exposing the socket. If you're unable to loosen the shell, insert a small screwdriver at the *press* point (figure 10). This will usually dislodge it.

3. Disconnect the old wire. When you remove the shell, the cardboard insulator usually remains in it. If it's still covering the socket, pull it off. Loosen the two screws that hold the lamp cord to the socket and pull the cord out from the bottom of the lamp. You may have to take the felt off the base of the lamp to access the cord.

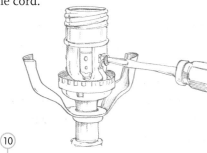

10

4. Feed the new cord, which should be 6 to 8 feet long, through the base and up through the lamp pipe and socket cap. With a sharp knife or razor blade, slit the insulation between the two wires, just wide enough to start the separation. Pull the two wires apart a couple of inches and strip about a ½ inch of insulation off each wire. Roll the wire between your thumb and index finger to twist all the little fine wires together. To protect the wires from strain when they are attached to the terminal screws, tie an underwriter's knot with the two ends (figure 11).

5. If you're using a polarized cord and plug (one prong is wider than the other), one wire is copper and the other is silver. Match the wires to the screws on the socket. This places the grounded side of the circuit on the outer portion of the socket—the part you could most easily touch by accident. I won't give you a course in electricity here, but this is a precaution to prevent shocks. Make sure the neutral wire of the cord (the wire with ridged plastic) connects to the silver socket terminal and the wide plug prong. The hot, or unmarked, wire connects to the brass socket terminal and the narrow plug prong.

6. Make sure there are no stray strands of wire and tighten the screws securely. Work the loose knot up as close to the bottom of the interior as possible, pull the slack out of the cord from the bottom, and replace the shell and insulator. You'll feel it snap into place as you push the shell into the cap.

7. Replace the plug with an automatic plug. To do this, squeeze the prongs together and pull the insides out (figure 12). Insert the end of the cord through the hole in the cover and, holding the prongs outward, force the cord as far as possible into the opening between the prongs. Squeeze the prongs together and push the mechanism back into the cover, seating it firmly. If the plug has one prong wider than the other and the cord has silver and copper-colored wires, the silver side attaches to the wide prong. (Don't worry if the lamp cord or the plug is not polarized; most aren't. Believe me, you won't electrocute anyone. There's no backward way to wire a single-socket lamp!)

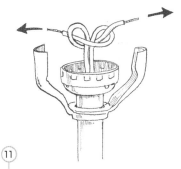

(11)

Tying an underwriter's knot

(12)

mary g

Artist Mary Ginn of Bothell, Washington, creates lampshades with handmade

paper and Japanese fibers. The paper is wrapped over wire armatures, which sit atop ceramic bases that are crafted by Ginn's husband. *Photo by Terry Reed.*

8. Replace the felt. Normally, you'll destroy the felt on the bottom of a table lamp when you rewire it. You can buy self-stick felt from suppliers or craft stores. Spread a coat of thick craft glue on the base and set the lamp on top of the felt. After the glue has dried, trim the excess close to the base with sharp scissors.

installing a flat cord switch

It's a good idea to install a flat cord switch if the socket on your lamp doesn't have one or if it's difficult to reach under the shade to turn the lamp on. You can purchase a flat cord switch from lamp suppliers or hardware stores.

materials
- Flat lamp cord
- Screwdriver
- Switch
- Cutting knife

1. Choose a convenient place along the lamp cord to install the switch. Use a screwdriver to unscrew the switch cover and separate the switch into two pieces.

2. With a cutting knife, slice a notch in the cord that is large enough to accommodate the center screw of the switch, then set the cord into the switch (figure 13).

3. Place the switch cover on the cord, making sure that both prongs of the switch pierce the same wire of the cord. If the lamp is polarized, the prongs must pierce the hot (unmarked) wire of the lamp cord.

4. Reattach the switch cover.

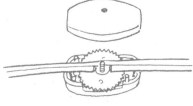

(13)

APPENDIX

glossary of terms

Bellows applicator: a small squirt bottle with a fine-point tip used for applying glue neatly.

Binding: a material, such as water-activated paper tape, yarn, thread, cord, or cotton twill, used to encase the raw edges of the styrene and paper and the top and bottom wires. Always use cotton or rayon-blend ribbons, because polyester repels glue.

Bottom wire ring: a simple wire hoop that supports and maintains the shape of the bottom of the shade.

Bulldog clips: clamps that are used to check the fit of a shade and to hold the shade in place as it dries after gluing.

Butterfly clip: a clip made of two pieces of wire that snap onto the lightbulb.

Cast iron loaders: objects that slip into the base of the lamp to add weight.

Clip adapter: a gadget that clips onto the bulb for lamps that don't have a harp.

Dimmer: a device connected to the lamp cord that varies the brightness of the bulb.

Felt: fabric attached to the bottom of a lamp base to prevent it from scratching a table's surface.

Finial: a plain or decorative fixture that screws onto the harp to hold the shade in place.

Fitter wire: a support that attaches a standard wire lampshade frame to the lamp.

Harp: a metal attachment that holds the lampshade above the bulb.

Lamp cord: the cord that comes up through the lamp base and connects directly to the socket. Brown, black, and white seem to be the standard colors, but the cord is also available from lamp suppliers in gold, clear, ivory, and silver.

Lamp pipe: a standard $\frac{3}{8}$-inch hollow pipe that comes in lengths ranging in 1-inch increments from 6 to 18 inches. It is available in nickel or brass plate with threaded ends. Threaded rod is also available in shorter lengths.

Lampshade frame: a frame usually made of galvanized steel, brass, or copper wire. Most frames are made by hand on shaped blocks, creating slight variation in the panel sizes. Lampshade frames are available from craft and sewing stores or from lamp suppliers.

Plug: prefitted prongs that provide the proper connection between the lamp and the source of electricity. If one prong is wider than the other, the plug is polarized and the wide prong should connect to the ridged wire on the lamp cord. You can purchase easy-to-install plugs that attach to the lamp cord.

Socket: a fixture that holds a bulb.

Socket riser/reducer: a device that screws into existing sockets to make the bulb sit higher or lower in the fixture.

Styrene: a translucent material used as a support for lampshades constructed with top and bottom rings. Pressure-sensitive styrene has a sticky side covered with peel-off paper that makes it easy to apply to decorative papers.

Switch: the device that turns the lamp on and off, so you don't have to plug and unplug the lamp each time. If the socket doesn't have a switch, you can buy a switch that attaches to the cord.

Top fitter wire ring: a device that supports and maintains the shape of the shade's top and consists of a fitter wire attached to a wire ring. Fitter wires can be flush with the top ring or recessed. Top rings attach the shade to the lamp with a variety of devices, including a washer top, bridge top, chimney top, or clip top.

Uno-bridge attachment: a fixture that screws onto the shell of the lamp socket. It can be used on a lamp in which the bulb hangs downward.

Vase cap: a cap that covers the opening at the top of a vase that is being converted into a lamp base. The caps come in a variety of sizes and have a hole in the center to accommodate the lamp pipe.

White glue: a fast-setting, archival glue, such as polyvinyl acetate (PVA). Suppliers also carry a brand called Quik, which many customers swear by.

pop-up lantern pattern

Photocopy this pattern at 100%. The final template should measure 1¼ in. x 6 in.

shadow lantern patterns

Photocopy the screen pattern at 200%. The final template should measure 5½ in. x 7 in.

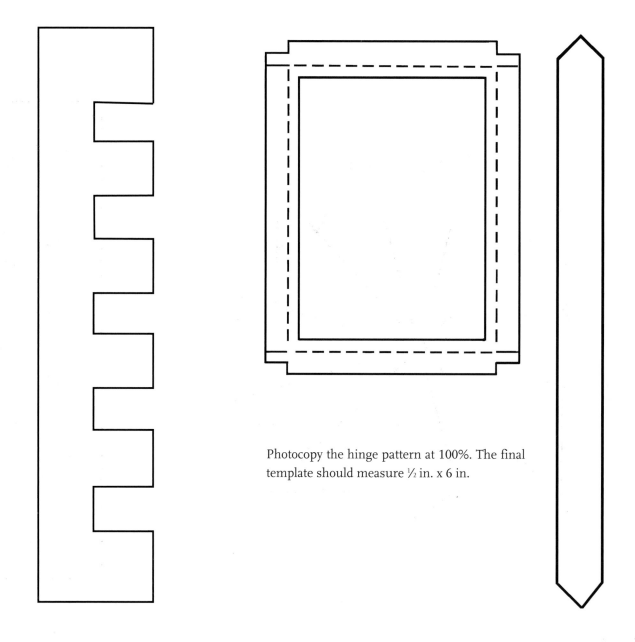

Photocopy the hinge pattern at 100%. The final template should measure ½ in. x 6 in.

spinning lantern patterns

Photocopy the pinwheel pattern at 200%. The final template should measure 8¾ in. by 8¾ in. from point to point.

Photocopy the cutout pattern at 300%. The final template should measure 4½ in. x 15 in.

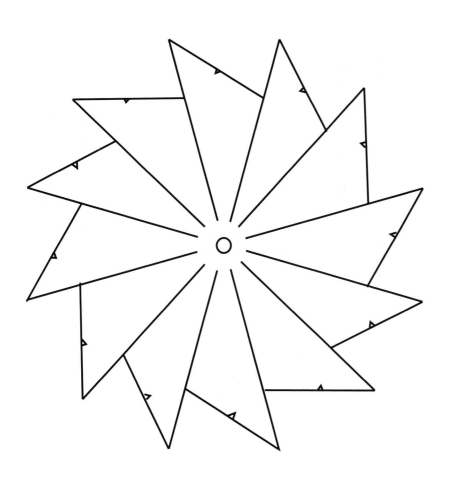

chochin lantern patterns

Photocopy the lamp rib pattern at 200%. The final template should measure 11 in. vertically.

Photocopy the shade pattern at 300%. The final template should measure 14½ in. vertically.

Photocopy the spoke pattern at 200%. The final template should measure 2¾ in. x 2¾ in.

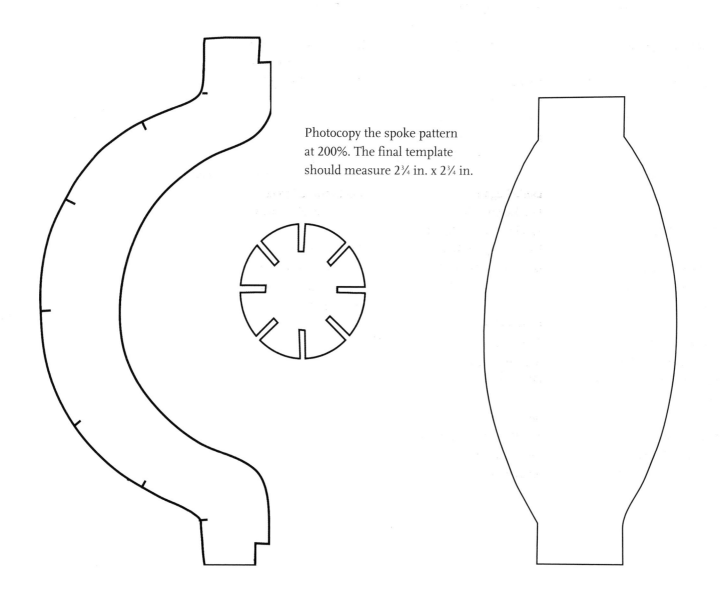

contributing artists

Béatrice Coron
372 Central Park West #20D
New York, NY 10025
www.beatricecoron.com
b@beatricecoron.com

Amanda Degener
1334 6th St. NE
Minneapolis, MN 55413
amanda_degener@mcad.edu

Ming Fay
830 Broadway 9th Fl.
New York, NY 10003
(212) 477-6508

Barbara Fletcher
(978) 667-2314
(978) 670-5290 fax
Paper3d@Hotmail.com
www.paperdimensions.com

Galbraith & Paul
307 North Third St.
Philadelphia, PA 19106
(215) 923-4632

Mary Ginn
20415 80th Ave. NE
Kenmore, WA 98028
BGINN3@Home.com

Helen Hiebert
618 NE Shaver St.
Portland, OR 97212
(503) 284-7987
HHiebert@aol.com
http://members.aol.com/
 hhiebert/html/

Kyoko Ibe
9-9 Higashinodan
Tenado cho Mukoshi
Kyoto, Japan 7617-0002
ibekyoko@mub.biglobe.ne.jp

Lanie Kagan
Luz Lampcraft
17 Little West 12th St.
New York, NY 10014
(212) 627-2875 FAX
(212) 255-1909

RESOLUTE
2101 9th Avenue
Seattle, WA 98121
(206) 343-9323

Janet St. Cyr
120 Pearson Hill Road1
Webster, NH 03303
(603) 648-2593

Ruth Timm
385 Ireland St.
West Chesterfield, MA 01084
(413) 296-8053
rltslt@aol.com

Jennifer Morrow Wilson
455 Eggemoggin Road
Deer Isle, ME 04650
(207) 348-6871
jmorrowwilson@acadia.net

Paul Wong
c/o Dieu Donne Papermill, Inc.
433 Broome Street
New York, NY 10013

Therese Zemlin
20 Grampian Way #1
Dorchester, MA 02125
(617) 288-9197

recommended reading

Bethmann, Laura Donnelly. *Nature Printing*. Pownal, VT: Storey Books, 2000.

Bryan Reid, Susan, Ed. *Lighting and Electricity*. Chicago, IL: St. Remy Press, 1997.

Buisson, Dominique. *The Art of Japanese Paper*. Paris, France: Finest S.A./Éditions Pierre Terrail, 1992.

Cargill, Katrin. *Lampshades*. New York, NY: Clarkson Potter Publishers, 1996.

Chatani, Masahiro. *Pop-Up Origamic Architecture*. Tokyo, Japan: Ondorisha Publishers, 1984.

Chatani, Masahiro, and Keiko Nakazawa. *Pop-Up Origami*. Tokyo, Japan: Ondorisha Publishers, 1994.

Christopher, F.J. *Lampshade Making*. New York, NY: Dover Publications, 1952.

Cusick, Dawn. *The Lampshade Book*. New York, NY: Sterling Publishing, 1996.

Davis, Jodie. *Crafting Lamps and Shades: Over 30 Easy, Inexpensive and Unique Projects to Light Up Your Home*. Iola, WI: Krause Publications, 1998.

Ekiguchi, Kunio, and Ruth S. McCreery. *Japanese Crafts and Customs*. New York, NY: Kodansha International, 1987.

Falkiner, Gabrielle. *Paper: An Inspirational Portfolio*. New York, NY: Watson-Guptill Publications, 1999.

Griffith, M.R. *The Lampshade Book*. London, UK: G. Bell and Sons, 1955.

Hiebert, Helen. *The Papermaker's Companion*. Pownal, VT: Storey Books, 2000.

Hiebert, Helen. *Papermaking with Plants*. Pownal, VT: Storey Books, 1998.

Isamu Noguchi. San Francisco, CA: Chronicle Books, 1985.

Jackson, Paul. *The Encyclopedia of Origami and Papercraft Techniques*. Philadelphia, PA: Running Press, 1991.

James, Angela. *The Handmade Book*. Pownal, VT: Storey Books, 2000.

Johnson, Pauline. *Creating with Paper*. Seattle, WA: University of Washington Press, 1958.

Kenyon, Scott Ormsbee, and Syndney Kenyon. *Lampshade Construction*. Concord, NH: The Lamp Shop, 1997.

Maurer-Mathison, Diane. *Paper Art*. New York, NY: Watson-Guptill Publications, 1997.

McKenzie, James W. *Antiques on the Cheap*. Pownal, VT: Storey Books, 1998.

Myerson, Jeremy, and Sylvia Katz. *Lamps and Lighting*. New York, NY: Van Nostrand Reinhold, 1990.

Ormsbee, Bee, and Scott Ormsbee Kenyon. *Lampshades: Basic Wraparound Construction and Cut and Pierced*. Concord, NH: The Lamp Shop, 2000.

Phillips, Derek. *Lighting*. London, England: Macdonald and Co., 1966.

Ramsay, Angela. *The Handmade Paper Book*. Pownal, VT: Storey Books, 1999.

Saddington, Marianne. *Making Your Own Paper*. Pownal, VT: Storey Books, 1992.

Shannon, Faith. *Paper Pleasures*. New York, NY: Weidenfeld and Nicolson, 1987.

Van Arsdale, Jay. *Shoji: How to Design, Build and Install Japanese Screens*. New York, NY: Kodansha International, 1988.

Yagi, Koji. *A Japanese Touch for Your Home*. New York, NY: Kodansha International, 1982.

supply sources

lampmaking supplies

The Lamp Shop
P.O. Box 3606
Concord, NH 03302
(603) 224-1603
www.lampshop.com

Victorian Classics
4128 N.E. Sandy Boulevard
Portland, OR 97212
(503) 282-7055

wholesale lamp parts (small minimum order)

Kirk's Lane Lamp Parts
P.O. Box 1073
Bensalem, PA 19020
(800) 355-5475
www.kirkslane.com

various kinds of small metal pieces and wires

Metalliferous
34 West 46th Street
New York, NY 10036
(212) 944-0909

bookbinding supplies

Bookmakers International
6701B Lafayette Avenue
Riverdale Park, MD 20737
(301) 927-7787

papermaking supplies

Dieu Donné Papermill
433 Broome Street
New York, NY 10013
(212) 226-0573
www.papermaking.org

Twinrocker Handmade Paper
P.O. Box 413
Brookston, IN 47923
(765) 563-3119
www.twinrocker.com

general art supplies

Dick Blick Art Materials
P.O. Box 1267
Galesburg, IL 61402-1267
(800) 828-4548
www.dickblick.com

Nasco
901 Janesville Avenue
P.O. Box 901
Fort Atkinson, WI 53538-0901
(800) 558-9595
www.enasco.com

papers

Loose Ends
P.O. Box 20310
Salem, OR 97307-0310
(503) 393-2348
www.4loosends.com

roscoflamex fire retardent

Dudley Theatrical
3401 Indiana Avenue
Winston-Salem, NC 27105
(336) 722-3255
www.dudleytheatrical.com

linen thread

Royalwood Ltd.
517 Woodville Road
Mansfield, OH 44907
(800) 526-1630
www.royalwoodltd.com

reed

Allen's Basketworks Inc.
P.O. Box 3217
Palm Springs, CA 92263
(800) 284-7333
www.allensbasketworks.com

Earth Guild
33 Haywood Street
Asheville, NC 28801
(800) 327-8448
www.earthguild.com

index

Acrylic, 11
Adhesives, 4, 31

Batiking, 7, 13
Beeswax, for translucence, 8
Blinds, accordion, 43–51

Candles
    pop-up lanterns, 25–27, 128
    safety, 23, 37
    shadow lanterns, 29–34, 128
    votive covers, 37–39
Chalk, 14
Chochin lanterns, 83–87, 130
Collages, 13, 19
Color, adding, 12–17
Coloring agents, 5
Coron, Bèatrice, 39
Cover-weight paper, 4
Crayon, 11, 13
Crumpling, 19
Cut-and-pierced technique, 7–8
Cutting, 7–8, 10

Degener, Amanda, 32
Dimension, adding, 18–21

Electricity
    safety, 116–19, 123
    wiring techniques, 123–26
Embossing, 19–20

Fay, Ming, 55
Fireproof materials, 119
Fletcher, Barbara, 5
Fold and dye, 13

Galbraith & Paul, 113
Glues, 4, 31
Grain, of paper, 3

Heat safety, 116–117

Ibe, Kyoko, 47
Inks, 4
Itajame, 13

Kagan, Lanie, 118

Lamps and lanterns
    chochin, 83–87, 130
    lamp bases, 121–23
    lightbulbs, 119–20
    luminaria, 71–73
    night-lights, 89–91
    pop-up, 25–27, 128
    shadow, 29–34, 128
    Shoji screen, 67
    sockets, 122–23
    spinning, 75–80, 129
    wall sconces, 93–95
    wiring, 123–26
Lampshades
    bulb clips, 101
    lacing holes, 111
    panel, 97–101
    proportion to base, 121
    re-covering, 107
    safety, 116–19
    terminology, 105
    wraparound, 103–12
Lanterns. See Lamps and lanterns
Layering, 9
Lightbulbs, 119–20
Lightfastness, 3
Luminaria, 71–73

Marbling, 14
Momigami, 19
Mosaic, paper, 51

Nature printing, 15
Night-lights, 89–91
Noguchi, Isamu, 35

Oil, for translucence, 9
Origami, 20

Paints, 4
Paper
    selecting, 2–5 (See also specific projects)
    heat safety, 116–17
Paste, 15, 59–60
Patchwork, 20
Patterns
    lampshade, 99
    templates, 128–30
Piercing, 7–8, 10
Pinwheels, 76
Pleats, accordion, 19, 26, 43–51
Pockets, paper, 20, 53–55
Pop-ups, 21, 25–27, 128
Punching, 11

RESOLUTE, 81
Right vs. wrong side of paper, 4
Room dividers, 57–60
Rope lights, 93
Rubber stamping, 16
Rubbing, 16

Safety
    candles, 23, 37
    lampshades, 116–19

wiring, 123
Sconces, 93–95
Scratch-through, 11
Screens, 57–60, 63–67
Shades, pocket, 53–55
Shadow lanterns, 29–34, 128
Sizing, defined, 3
Sockets, lamp, 122–23
Spinning lanterns, 75–80, 129
St. Cyr, Janet, 10
Stained glass effect, 11
Stenciling, 16–17, 30
Suminagashi, 14
Switches, 126

Tapes, adhesive, 4
Texture, adding, 18–21
Text-weight paper, 4
Tie-dying, 17
Timm, Ruth, 21
Translucence, enhancing, 6–11

Vase caps, 122
Vellum, printed, 11
Votive covers, 37–39

Wall sconces, 93–95
Watermarks, on luminaria, 73
Weaving, 21
Wet-strength, 3
Wilson, Jennifer Morrow, 15
Window coverings, 43–51, 53–55, 63–67
Wiring techniques, 123–26
Wong, Paul, 61

Zemlin, Therese, 95

53 2260R1 7323
FS
07/10 30800-25 UA